← Laila's sister

Sarah Lynk

Sarah Lynk inherited a love of cooking from her Lebanese parents. There is a saying among the Lebanese that if they're not cooking food, they're talking about food. Sarah's gift of hospitality and her reputation for preparing delicious meals has followed her wherever she goes, She is delighted to have teamed up with the internationally respected photographer Sherman Hines, to bring you this special book of recipes. Sarah is married with three wonderful children, and lives in Halifax, Nova Scotia. She has spent 18 years as a nurse and 10 years as a successful real estate agent.

Sherman Hines

Sherman Hines has over 65 photographic books published featuring his extraordinary images, and has merited such recognition as Canadian Photographer of the Year, a Fellowship in The American Society of Photographers and an honorary doctorate from St. Mary's and two gold medals of excellence. His hometown of Liverpool, Nova Scotia is the location of "The Sherman Hines Museum of Photography.,"

Scenic Nova Scotia COOKBOOK

Nova Scotian & Middle Eastern Foods for All Seasons

"No matter where I serve my guests,
it seems they like my kitchen best."

Text and Recipes by Sarah Lynk
Photographs by Sherman Hines

Dedication

This book is dedicated to my mother and father,
Dehbieh and Mahfoth Joseph,
who bequeathed to me the joys of hospitality and the
rich heritage of Middle Eastern traditions.

Acknowledgements

My relationship with Sherman Hines goes back many years. I first made his acquaintance at a wedding, where—naturally enough—he was taking photographs. By chance, a few years later I met his lovely wife, Andrea, who became interested in my ongoing crusade of teaching breadmaking. And as often happens, baking (and breaking) bread together developed into a long friendship between our families.

Years later I developed and contributed the recipes for Sherman's Hunter's Guide. This sparked Sherman's interest in publishing a cookbook. Many friends expressed enthusiasm at the idea of combining his photographs with my recipes, and thus began our project in earnest. So to all those dear friends around the world who have been waiting for the finished product, cook, eat and enjoy!

Introduction

I was born above a bakery in the small town of Bridgewater, Nova Scotia. My parents were newly-arrived immigrants from Lebanon, and the tantalising aromas wafting upstairs, coupled with my parent's rich Middle Eastern cooking traditions gave an early birth to my lifelong passion for food. My first memories are those of following my nose into my mother's kitchen, where steaming pots of lamb stew (yuknee), and lentils and rice (mjudraa) could always be found simmering on top of the wood stove. During the Depression, my parent's home was always open to anyone who needed a meal, despite the fact that our family survived on the fruits and vegetables from our large garden, and what my Papa could earn as a peddler along the south shore of Nova Scotia. Following their example, I have tried to continue this gift of Lebanese hospitality. It is a blessing, perhaps, that Middle Eastern cuisine is not only mouth-watering and nutritious, but inexpensive to prepare. A few dollars wisely spent can feed a multitude—and I often do!

To my delight, this gift of hospitality has passed on to my own children. The recipes in this book have been handed down from family and friends, and have been tried and tasted many times over. However, compiling the recipes has been a learning experience for me, as I learned to cook at my mother's knee, in the best tradition of "a little of this, a pinch of that."

I encourage you to use these recipes merely as a starting point, and to experiment as your confidence grows and your taste buds unfold.

Always strive for excellence, but don't be afraid to make mistakes. Therein lies the secret of a good cook. My cardinal rule of cooking is to use the best and freshest ingredients possible. Nothing brings out the essence of taste as do the first vegetables of spring, or fresh fish and meats, or ripening fruits. Butter gives the richest flavour to baked goods, extra-virgin olive oil has no equal, and canola oil is superb for breadmaking. Freshly prepared foods also make the difference. Plan ahead. This simplifies things wonderfully. Think today what tomorrow will bring, and try to cook in stages.

When expecting guests, I often write out my menus well ahead of time, then work backwards, setting my table early, preparing desserts first, appetisers next, and entrées last.

Many of my closest friendships have developed through the sharing of food. Everyone seems to love a gift from the kitchen, and the art of hospitality itself is rooted in the breaking of bread. My children have often remarked on the diverse and inspirational guests from around the globe who have graced our table.

These moments of sharing food and friendship represent some of my most treasured memories, and continue to be an education for us all. Truly the joys of cooking are in the offering, however simple.

"My home is the home of peace. My home is the home of joy and delight.

My home is the home of laughter and exultation.

Whosoever enters through the portals of this home,

must go forth with gladsome heart."

Contents

"Cast thy bread upon the waters: for thou shalt find it after many days."
BIBLE

Bread making is easy, creative and oh so satisfying! Where else can one double one's investment in only a few short hours! And making bread by the refrigerator method controls the time factor, thus simplifying bread making.

Once you've mastered the basics of bread making, you can have the enjoyment of creating your own endless variations. The possibilities for innovation match only how much you challenge your imagination.

Steps to Bread Making

1. Place warm water in a large bowl. Add molasses or sugar. Then sprinkle yeast over the water. Let rest for 10 minutes. The yeast is proofed or active when it begins to bubble.

2. Add all the ingredients except flour. Gradually add the flours, stirring vigorously to make a fairly stiff dough. Start this process with a big wooden spoon, then when this becomes too difficult, use your right hand to work in all traces of flour. Do this with an open shut motion of the right hand.

3. Turn dough on to a lightly floured board. Begin to knead, adding flour as necessary to prevent sticking. Firstly, pick up the underside of the ball of dough farthest from you, folding it in half and bringing it towards you. Push it lightly and quickly away from you, using the heel of your hands. Pull it toward you again with your two palms. Repeat these two motions (folding and pushing) turning a quarter turn each time, and adding more flour as necessary. Knead until the dough is smooth and elastic, about 8 minutes.

4. *Important tip:* The dough should be flexible. Do not add too much flour. Too stiff a dough makes a heavy, tough bread.

5. For the straight method:
• use half the amount of yeast called for in the refrigerator method.

• Cover dough with a plastic bag. Let the dough rise till doubled in bulk in a large bowl. When doubled, punch down, Let rise till doubled a second time. Punch down and shape into pans.
    To Shape: make two buns per loaf pan, filling well greased pans about 2/3 full. To make buns, squeeze out all bubbles by flattening a piece of dough on a lightly floured surface, form into ball by gently pulling the top surface towards the underside, pinching the seams.
    Put the buns, seam side down in a well greased loaf pan. Let rise until size is doubled. Dough is adequately risen when after poking two fingers gently into it, the indentation remains. Bake at 375°F (190°C) for about
45 minutes or until medium brown.

6. Refrigeration Method (I use this almost exclusively) An alternative to the straight methods is the refrigerator method. After mixing and kneading dough, place in a large plastic bag leaving lots of room for expansion, expel air, then tie end of bag. Place in fridge. Use within two or three days. Remove from fridge. Punch down and shape into well-greased loaf pans filling to 2/3 full. this methods simplifies the time factor significantly. Let rise until doubled in a warm place for one and
a half to two hours.
    When risen, brush tops with beaten egg, sprinkle with sesame seeds or poppy seeds. Bake at 375°F (190°C) for about 45 minutes. Remove from over, turn out on rack to cool. Place in plastic bags and store.
    To make bread by refrigerator methods,use an additional two tablespoons of yeast when mixing up the bread.
    Some variations: Mashed potatoes with the potato water adds greatly to the lightness and flavor.Also add mashed, overripe bananas to the bread batter.

7. When you come to bake the bread place a jellyroll pan in the bottom of the over, pre-heat oven to 375°F (190°C). Place bread in pre-heated oven and put a cup of hot water in jellyroll pan and proceed to bake bread for 45 minutes. Steam created helps bread to rise and improves texture and crust.

Breads

With the wide variety of speciality breads available in the supermarkets these days, you may wonder why some of us continue to bake our own. The answer lies both in the heavenly taste and aroma of bread fresh from the oven, and in the immense satisfaction derived from creating something so impressive from a few simple ingredients. After all, how else can one double one's investment in only a few short hours! Once you've mastered the basics of breadmaking, you can develop your own variations—the possibilities are limited only by your imagination.

Basic Sweet Dough

This sweet dough, enriched with eggs, is used to make many good things—coffee rings, cinnamon rolls, sticky buns, and just about anything else that fires your imagination. The quantities given here are enough to make four batches of each of the following sweet-dough recipes.

3 cups (750 ml) warm water

1 cup (250 ml) white sugar

3 tablespoons (40 ml) dry yeast

1 cup (250 ml) very soft butter

4 eggs, beaten

2 teaspoons (10 ml) sea salt

8–10 cups (2–2.5 L) all-purpose flour

Combine the water and sugar in a large bowl, stirring to dissolve the sugar. Sprinkle the yeast over top and leave for 10 minutes to proof. Beat in the butter, eggs, and salt. Gradually mix in 6–7 cups of flour, stirring vigorously with a wooden spoon.

When the dough becomes too stiff to stir, use your hands to mix in another cup of flour. Turn the dough out on to a lightly floured surface, scraping down the sides of the bowl. Knead for 3–4 minutes, until smooth and elastic, adding small amounts of flour as necessary.

Place the dough in a large plastic bag and refrigerate for at least eight hours and up to three days, punching down occasionally. Use in any of the recipes that follow.

Grainy Wheat Loaves or Pan Buns

MAKES 3 LOAVES + 1 DOZEN BUNS

Grainy wheat bread is my daily bread—rich in flavour and delicious toasted. It also freezes beautifully, and you can use part of the dough to make pan buns. Simply take a portion of the kneaded dough and form it into a long cylinder. Using a sharp knife, divide the dough into large egg-sized pieces. Roll into balls, pinching the seams and turning the ends under. Place the rolls in a 10-inch (25-cm) round greased pan, seam-side down, cover with a cloth and leave in a warm place for 30–60 minutes, until doubled in size. Glaze as directed below and bake in a preheated 375°F (190°C) oven for 35–50 minutes.

- 4 cups (1 L) warm water
- 1/2 cup (125 ml) molasses
- 2 tablespoons (25 ml) dry yeast
- 1 1/2 tablespoons (20 ml) sea salt
- 1/3 cup (80 ml) canola oil
- 1/2 cup (125 ml) cracked wheat
- 2 cups (500 ml) whole wheat flour
- 8–10 cups (2–2.5 L) all-purpose flour

To glaze:
- 1–2 eggs, beaten
- sesame or poppy seeds

Combine the water and molasses in a large bowl. Sprinkle the yeast over top and leave for 10 minutes to proof. Add the salt, oil, and cracked wheat, and stir vigorously with a wooden spoon, gradually adding the whole wheat flour and about 5 cups of the all-purpose flour.

When the dough becomes too stiff to stir, use your hands to mix in about 2 more cups of flour. Turn the dough out on to a lightly floured surface, scraping down the sides of the bowl until all traces of flour disappear. Knead for 8 minutes, until smooth and elastic, adding small amounts of flour as necessary. Place the dough in a large plastic bag and refrigerate for at least eight hours, and up to three days, punching down occasionally.

Remove from the refrigerator and divide in four pieces. Shape into loaves or reserve two buns per pan, as directed above, and place in well-greased loaf pans, filling them no more than two-thirds full. Leave in a warm place to rise for 1–1 1/2 hours, until doubled in size.

Preheat the oven to 375°F (180°C). Brush the risen loaves with the beaten egg and sprinkle with sesame or poppy seeds. Bake up to three loaves at a time for 45–50 minutes on the second-lowest oven rack. Invert the baked loaves on to a rack to cool.

Dark Rye Bread

MAKES 4 LARGE LOAVES

This dense and velvety-textured bread is terrific served with soups and makes hearty sandwiches. By dividing the dough into two large "buns" per pan, you end up with nice compact loaves.

4 cups (1 L) potato water
1/2 cup (125 ml) molasses
3 tablespoons (40 ml) dry yeast
1/3 cup (80 ml) canola oil
1 tablespoon (15 ml) sea salt
2 cups (500 ml) dark rye flour
1 cup (250 ml) cooked rolled oats
approximately 8 cups (2 L) unbleached flour

To glaze:

1–2 eggs, beaten
sesame or poppy seeds

Combine the potato water and molasses in a large bowl. Sprinkle the yeast over top and leave for 10 minutes to proof. Add the oil, salt, rye flour, and rolled oats, and stir vigorously with a wooden spoon, gradually adding about 5 cups of the unbleached flour.

When the dough becomes too stiff to stir, use your hands to mix in about 2 more cups of flour. Turn the dough out on to a lightly floured surface, scraping down the sides of the bowl. Knead for 8 minutes, until smooth and elastic, adding small amounts of flour as necessary. Place the dough in a large plastic bag and refrigerate for at least eight hours, and up to three days, punching down occasionally.

Remove from the refrigerator and divide in eight pieces. Shape into large buns and place two buns, seam-side down and end to end, in each well-greased loaf pan, filling them no more than two-thirds full. Leave in a warm place to rise for 1–1 1/2 hours, until doubled in size.

Preheat the oven to 375°F (190°C). Glaze the risen loaves with the beaten egg and sprinkle with sesame or poppy seeds. Bake up to three loaves at a time for 45–50 minutes on the second-lowest oven rack. Invert the baked loaves on to a rack to cool.

Pumpernickel Bread

MAKES 3–4 LOAVES

The secret ingredient in this dark and delicious bread is the cocoa. The bran adds a healthy boost of fibre.

4 cups (2 L) warm water

1/2 cup (125 ml) molasses

3 tablespoons (40 ml) dry yeast

1/4 cup (50 ml) canola oil

1 tablespoon (15 ml) salt

1/2 cup (125 ml) cocoa

1 cup (250 ml) bran

2 cups (500 ml) rye flour

6–7 cups (1.5–1.75 L) all-purpose flour

To glaze:

1–2 eggs, beaten

sesame or poppy seeds

Combine the water and molasses in a large bowl. Sprinkle the yeast over top and leave for 10 minutes to proof. Add the oil, salt, cocoa, bran, and rye flour, and stir vigorously with a wooden spoon, gradually adding about 5 cups of the all-purpose flour.

When the dough becomes too stiff to stir, use your hands to mix in another cup of flour. Turn the dough out on to a lightly floured surface, scraping down the sides of the bowl. Knead for 8 minutes, until smooth and elastic, adding small amounts of flour as necessary. Place the dough in a large plastic bag and refrigerate for at least eight hours, and up to three days, punching down occasionally.

Remove from the refrigerator and divide in six to eight pieces. Shape into large buns and place two buns, seam-side down and end to end, in each well-greased loaf pan, filling them no more than two-thirds full. Leave in a warm place to rise for 1–1 1/2 hours, until doubled in size.

Preheat the oven to 375˚F (190˚C). Glaze the risen loaves with the beaten egg and sprinkle with sesame or poppy seeds. Bake up to three loaves at a time for 45–50 minutes on the second-lowest oven rack. Invert the baked loaves on to a rack to cool.

Tea Ring

SERVES 4–6

This festive ring will be appreciated any time of year, but it is particularly nice at Christmas and Easter. For special occasions, I like to garnish it with glazed or candied fruit. I make many of these rings each year during the holidays and give them as gifts to grateful friends.

1/4 recipe of Basic Sweet Dough (page 10)

For the filling:

3 tablespoon (15 ml) soft butter

1/4 cup (50 ml) brown sugar

1 tablespoon (15 ml) cinnamon

1/2 cup (125 ml) raisins

For the glaze:

2/3 cup (160 ml) icing sugar

2 tablespoons (25 ml) freshly squeezed lemon juice
glazed or candied fruit, to garnish

Roll out the chilled dough on a lightly floured surface to form a 9 x 20-inch (23 x-50-cm) rectangle. Spread with the soft butter to within 1/2 inch (1 cm) of the edges. Combine the sugar and cinnamon and sprinkle evenly over the butter. Next scatter the raisins over top.

Dampen the edge of the dough with warm water or milk and roll it up tightly lengthways, pinching the edges to seal. Place the roll, seam-side down, on a greased baking sheet, shaping it into a ring and pinching the ends together to seal.

Using sharp scissors, slice the ring at 2-inch (5-cm) intervals, cutting through the dough to within 1/2 inch (1 cm) of the bottom. Cover with a clean cloth and leave in a warm place for 45–60 minutes, until doubled in bulk.

Preheat the oven to 350°F (180°C). Bake the ring for 25 minutes, until lightly browned. Meanwhile, beat together the icing sugar and lemon to make the glaze. Remove the baked ring from the oven, transfer to a cooling rack and spread lightly with the glaze. Garnish with candied fruit.

Cheese and Herb Rolls

MAKES 12

These savory rolls are wonderful served with soup and salad. Mix up a batch in the morning and have them fresh from the oven at lunch. Zattar is a mixed spice containing sesame seeds. It can be bought at Middle Eastern speciality stores and adds a lovely flavour and texture to bread.

2 cups (500 ml) warm water

1/3 cup (80 ml) white sugar

2 tablespoons (25 ml) dry yeast

1/3 cup (80 ml) butter, softened

2 eggs, beaten

1 tablespoon (15 ml) salt

2 cups (500 ml) grated sharp Cheddar cheese

3 tablespoons (40 ml) Zattar

2 hot jalapeño peppers, chopped very finely

2 small hot peppers, chopped very finely

1 cup (250 ml) finely chopped fresh parsley

2 large onions, chopped very finely

1 cup (250 ml) whole wheat flour

approximately 5 cups (1.25 L) all-purpose flour

Combine the water and sugar in a large bowl. Sprinkle the yeast over top and leave for 10 minutes to proof. Beat in the butter, eggs, and salt. Stir in the grated cheese, spices, chopped peppers, parsley, and onion. Gradually mix in the whole wheat flour and 3–4 cups of all-purpose flour, stirring vigorously with a wooden spoon, and switching to your hands once the mixture becomes too stiff.

Turn the dough out on to a lightly floured surface, scraping down the sides of the bowl. Knead for 6–8 minutes, until smooth and elastic, adding small amounts of flour as necessary. Place the dough back in the bowl, cover with a clean cloth and leave in a warm place to rise for 1–2 hours, until doubled in bulk.

Punch down the dough and turn out on to a lightly floured surface. Shape into a long cylinder and then, using a sharp knife, divide in twelve pieces. Shape into rolls and place in a well-greased muffin tin. Leave to rise again until doubled in size.

Preheat the oven to 350°F (180°C). Bake for 30 minutes and then invert the baked rolls on to a rack to cool.

Sticky Buns

MAKES 8–12

The sweet spicy fragrance of these sticky treats will everybody in the kitchen to see what's baking.

1/4 recipe of Basic Sweet Dough (page 10)

For the filling:
1/4 cup (50 ml) butter, softened
1 cup (250 ml) brown sugar
1 tablespoon (15 ml) cinnamon
1/2 cup (125 ml) raisins
1/2 cup (125 ml) chopped walnuts

Generously grease a 10-inch (25-cm) deep square or round pan.

Roll out the chilled dough on a lightly floured surface to form a rectangle about 1/2-inch (1-cm) thick. Spread generously with the butter, reserving 2 tablespoons. Combine 1/2 cup of the sugar with the cinnamon and sprinkle evenly over the dough. Next scatter half the raisins and nuts over top.

Dampen the edge of the dough with warm water or milk and roll it up tightly lengthways, pinching the edges to seal. Using a sharp knife, slice the roll in 8–12 pieces.

Meanwhile, melt the 2 tablespoons of butter in a small saucepan and stir in the remaining sugar, raisins, and nuts. Spread this mixture in the bottom of the greased pan. Arrange the dough slices, cut-sides down, in the pan. Cover with a clean cloth and leave in a warm place for 45–60 minutes, until doubled in bulk.

Preheat the oven to 350°F (180°C). Bake the buns for 30 minutes, then remove from the oven and invert on to a cooling rack. Leave for 10 minutes to allow the syrup to drain over the buns.

Yummy Raisin Bread

MAKES 3–4 LOAVES

Toasted raisin bread is a favourite treat during the cold winter months. Finely chopped oranges add a special flavour to this bread, which I've frequently heard described as "simply the best I've ever eaten." This dough rises at room temperature, and requires only two risings.

4 cups (1 L) raisins

4 medium-sized oranges, chopped finely

1 cup (250 ml) white sugar

2 cups (500 ml) boiling water

1 cup (250 ml) warm water

6 tablespoons (90 ml) dry yeast

1 cup (250 ml) butter, softened

4 eggs, beaten

2 tablespoons (25 ml) salt

8–10 cups (2–2.5 L) all-purpose flour

To glaze:

2 cups (500 ml) icing sugar

1/4 cup (50 ml) freshly squeezed lemon juice

Combine the raisins, chopped oranges, and 1 cup of sugar in a saucepan. Pour 2 cups of boiling water over top, stir briskly and set aside to cool.

Meanwhile, combine the warm water and sugar in a large bowl. Sprinkle the yeast over top and leave for 10 minutes to proof. Beat in the butter, eggs, and salt. Beat in the cooled fruit mixture and gradually mix in 6–7 cups of flour, stirring vigorously with a wooden spoon.

When the dough becomes too stiff to stir, use your hands to mix in another cup of flour. Turn the dough out on to a lightly floured surface, scraping down the sides of the bowl. Knead for 3–4 minutes, until smooth and elastic, adding small amounts of flour as necessary to make a soft dough. Place the dough back in the bowl, cover with a clean cloth and leave in a warm place to rise for 2 hours, until doubled in bulk.

Punch down the dough and turn out on to a lightly floured surface. Divide in six to eight pieces. Shape into large buns and place two buns, seam-side down in each well-greased loaf pan, filling them no more than two-thirds full. Leave in a warm place to rise for 1–1 1/2 hours, until doubled in size.

Preheat the oven to 350°F (180°C). Bake up to three loaves at a time for 45–50 minutes on the second-lowest oven rack. Beat together the icing sugar and lemon juice to make the glaze. Invert the baked loaves on to a rack to cool, and drizzle with the glaze.

Cakes
Cookies, Muffins & Squares

Nova Scotians are known for their hospitality, which often includes a pot of steaming fresh coffee and a generous slice of homemade cake or a plate of biscuits or cookies.

Peanut Butter Cookies

MAKES 1 DOZEN

These are a favourite any time of year. Use good quality natural peanut butter for the most flavourful results.

1/2 cup (125 ml) butter, softened
1/2 cup (125 ml) peanut butter
1/2 cup (125 ml) white sugar
1/2 cup (125 ml) brown sugar
1 egg, beaten
1 cup (250 ml) all-purpose flour
1 teaspoon (5 ml) baking soda

Preheat the oven to 350°F (180°C).

Cream the butter and peanut butter together with the sugars. Beat in the egg and then fold in the flour and soda, mixing well. Roll the dough between your lightly floured hands into small balls. Arrange 1 inch (2.5 cm) apart on an ungreased baking sheet, and flatten gently using the back of a fork. Bake for 8–10 minutes. Leave for 2–3 minutes before transferring to a rack to cool.

Gingersnaps

MAKES 2 DOZEN

These make great lunch-box or picnic treats.

1 cup (250 ml) molasses
1/2 cup (125 ml) vegetable shortening
1/4 cup (50 ml) butter
1/3 cup (80 ml) brown sugar
2 teaspoons (10 ml) baking soda
1 tablespoon (15 ml) ground ginger
3 1/2 cups (875 ml) all-purpose flour

Lightly grease a baking sheet and preheat the oven to 350°F (180°C).

Combine all the ingredients except for the flour in a large, heavy-based saucepan. Bring to a boil, stirring constantly, and then remove from the heat and allow to cool. Add the flour, stirring well to combine. Knead to form a stiff dough, and then turn out on to a floured surface. Roll out to a 1/4-inch (5-mm) thickness and cut into small rounds, arranging them 1 inch (2.5 cm) apart on the baking sheet. Bake for 8–10 minutes. Leave for 2–3 minutes before transferring to rack to cool.

Rich Hot Milk Cake with Fudge Frosting

MAKES TWO 9-INCH (23-CM) CAKES

This delicious desert cake is easy to make and freezes beautifully.

6 eggs

3 cups (750 ml) white sugar

1 1/2 cups (375 ml) whole milk

2/3 cup (180 ml) butter

3 cups (750 ml) all-purpose flour

1 tablespoon (15 ml) baking powder

2 cups (500 ml) toasted coconut and/or chopped pecans

For the frosting:

1 1/2 cups (500 ml) brown sugar

2 tablespoons (25 ml) cream

2 tablespoons (25 ml) butter

Generously grease and flour two 9-inch (23-cm) springform tube pans and preheat the oven to 325°F (170°C).

Beat the eggs in a large mixing bowl until light and foamy. Gradually add the sugar, beating constantly until light, creamy, and lemon-yellow in colour. Combine the milk and butter in a small saucepan and heat until scalded. Sieve together the flour and baking powder. Gradually add the milk and flour to the egg mixture, alternating between the two, and folding in gently until mixed thoroughly.

Spoon the batter into the prepared cake pans and bake in the centre of the oven for 40–45 minutes, until the cakes feel springy when pressed lightly. Remove from the pans and immediately sprinkle with the coconut and/or pecans.

Meanwhile, combine the frosting ingredients in a small saucepan and simmer for 5 minutes over a medium–low heat, stirring frequently. Sprinkle the cakes with the coconut and/or pecans, and then pour the frosting over top, and set them under a preheated broiler for a few minutes, watching carefully to make sure they don't burn. Leave to cool for 10 minutes and then remove sides of pans and transfer to a rack to finish cooling.

My Favourite Birthday Cake

SERVES 6–8

This cake has a fun chocolate ripple running through it. Make it for somebody's birthday—or better yet, have somebody make it for yours!

- 1 cup (250 ml) butter, softened
- 2 cups (500 ml) white sugar
- 3 eggs, beaten
- 3 cups (750 ml) all-purpose flour
- 2 teaspoon (10 ml) baking powder
- 1 cup (250 ml) blend cream
- 1/2 tablespoon (10 ml) vanilla
- 3 tablespoons (40 ml) grated lemon o
- 1/4 teaspoon (1 ml) baking soda

For the chocolate syrup:

- 2 squares unsweetened chocolate, cho
- 1 teaspoon (5 ml) vanilla
- 1/2 cup (125 ml) white sugar
- 1/2 cup (125 ml) corn syrup
- 1/2 cup (125 ml) cream
- 1 tablespoon (15 ml) butter
- 1/2 tablespoon (10 ml) vanilla

[handwritten note: omit 1/2 TBSP vanilla see pg 97]

Grease and flour a 10-inch (25-cm) bundt pan and preheat the oven to 325°F (190°C).

Combine the ingredients for the chocolate syrup, except for the butter and vanilla, in a small saucepan. Cook over a low heat, stirring frequently, for about 20 minutes. Remove from the heat and stir in the butter and vanilla. Set aside to cool.

In a large mixing bowl, cream the butter and sugar until light and fluffy. Gradually add the eggs, beating well. Sieve together the flour, baking powder, and stir into the butter mixture with the cream, until mixed well. Stir in the orange zest and vanilla.

Pour half the batter into the prepared pan. Spoon the chocolate syrup into the remaining batter and pour the chocolate syrup in a thin stream into the cake batter in the bowl. Swirl to marble the dark batter through the batter. Bake for 1 hour, or until a toothpick inserted into the centre of the cake comes out clean.

Black Forest Chocolate Cake

SERVES 6–8

This cake never goes out of style and is always a hit with chocolate lovers.

3/4 cup (175 ml) butter, softened

2 cups (500 ml) white sugar

3 eggs

2 teaspoons (10 ml) vanilla

3 squares unsweetened chocolate, melted

2 3/4 cups (675 ml) all-purpose flour

1 1/2 teaspoons (7 ml) baking soda

1 1/3 cups (330 ml) water

For the frosting:

2 cups (500 ml) whipping cream

1/3 cup (80 ml) white sugar

1/4 cup (50 ml) cocoa

2 teaspoons (10 ml) instant coffee

For the cherry garnish:

1 can of Bing cherries, drained with juices reserved

2 tablespoons (25 ml) cornstarch

Grease and flour three 8-inch (20-cm) round cake pans and preheat the oven to 325°F (170°C).

In a large mixing bowl, cream together the butter and sugar until light and fluffy. Add the eggs, one at a time, beating well after each addition. Stir in the vanilla and melted chocolate. Sieve together the flour and baking soda and gradually fold into the batter, alternating with the water.

Divide the batter between the three cake pans and bake for 25–35 minutes, until the cakes spring back when pressed lightly. Cool for 10 minutes in the pans, and then carefully invert on to racks to cool completely.

To make the frosting, mix together the whipping cream, sugar, cocoa, and instant coffee in a large bowl and refrigerate for at least 3 hours, until well chilled. Beat until thick and light, then use it to sandwich the three cake layers together, reserving enough to frost the top.

Garnish with the cherry mixture, which is made by mixing the cornstarch with the reserved cherry juice and heating it over a low heat until smooth and thickened. Stir the cherries in and leave to cool before using.

Apple Sauce Loaf

MAKES 3 LOAVES

This cake tastes as good as any dark fruit cake, without leaving you feeling heavy and dissipated! Make one for yourself, one for the freezer, and one for a friend.

- 1 cup (250 ml) butter, softened
- 2 cups (500 ml) white sugar
- 4 eggs, beaten
- 1 tsp (5 ml) baking soda, 1/2 tsp baking powder
- 1/2 cup (125 ml) hot water
- 2 cups (500 ml) apple sauce
- grated zest of 2 lemons and 2 oranges
- 4 cups (1 L) all-purpose flour
- 2 teaspoons (10 ml) ground cinnamon
- 1 teaspoon (5 ml) ground cloves
- 1/2 teaspoon (2 ml) freshly grated nutmeg
- 6 cups (1.5 L) raisins
- 6 cups (1.5 L) dried currants

Grease and flour three 5 x 9-inch (13 x 23-cm) loaf pans and preheat the oven to 325°F (170°C).

In a large mixing bowl, cream together the butter and sugar until light and fluffy, and then gradually add the eggs, beating well after each addition. Dissolve the baking soda in the hot water and mix with the apple sauce. Stir into the butter mixture and add the lemon and orange zest. Sieve together the flour and spices and fold into the batter, making sure to incorporate all the ingredients. Fold in the raisins and currants.

Spoon the batter into the prepared loaf pans and cover with lightly greased foil. Place a pan filled with boiling water on the bottom rack of the oven, and bake the loaves on the second-lowest rack for 1 1/2 hours, until the loaves are firm to the touch. Remove the foil 20 minutes before the loaves are done. Leave in the pans for 10–15 minutes, and then carefully invert on to a rack to cool.

Cinnamon Loaf

MAKES 1 LOAF

This is a wonderful cake to have on hand when friends drop by for coffee. Buttermilk makes it nice and moist.

1/2 cup (125 ml) butter, softened

1 cup (250 ml) white sugar

2 eggs, beaten

2 teaspoons (10 ml) vanilla

1 3/4 cups (425 ml) all-purpose flour

1 teaspoon (5 ml) baking powder

1/2 teaspoon (2 ml) baking soda

1/2 cup (125 ml) buttermilk—or
1/2 cup (125 ml) whole milk soured with 1 teaspoon
(5 ml) vinegar

1 cup (250 ml) chopped walnuts

3 tablespoons (40 ml) brown sugar

1 tablespoon (15 ml) ground cinnamon

Grease and flour a 5 x 9-inch (13 x 23-cm) loaf pan and preheat the oven to 325°F (170°C).

In a large mixing bowl, cream together the butter and white sugar until light and fluffy. Gradually add the eggs, beating well after each addition. Stir in the vanilla. Sieve together the flour, baking powder, and soda, and fold into the batter, alternating with the buttermilk until incorporated. Fold in the chopped walnuts.

In a small bowl, mix together the brown sugar and cinnamon. Spoon one-third of the batter into the prepared loaf pan, then sprinkle half the cinnamon sugar evenly over top. Add another third of the batter and sprinkle with the remaining cinnamon sugar. Pour the remaining batter into the pan, and then zigzag a knife through the batter, which will swirl the cinnamon sugar throughout the batter.

Bake on the second-highest oven rack for 45 minutes. Leave in the pan for 10–15 minutes, and then carefully invert on to a rack to cool.

Blueberry Muffins

MAKES 1 DOZEN

These can be made using cranberries instead of blueberries, or a combination of both. If using cranberries, substitute orange zest for the lemon zest. The glaze keep the muffins moist and adds a boost of flavour.

1 1/2 cups (375 ml) all-purpose flour
1/2 cup (125 ml) white sugar
2 teaspoons (10 ml) baking powder
1/4 teaspoon (1 ml) baking soda
1/3 cup (80 ml) butter, cubed
1/2 cup (125 ml) whole milk
2 eggs, beaten
1 cup (250 ml) fresh or frozen blueberries

For the glaze:

freshly squeezed juice of one lemon with
3/4 cup (150 ml) white sugar

Generously grease a 12-cup muffin pan and preheat the oven to 375°F (180°C).

In a large mixing bowl, sieve together the flour, sugar, baking powder and soda. Rub in the butter until the mixture resembles peas-sized crumbs. Add the milk and beaten eggs all at once, and stir until the dry ingredients are just moistened. Fill the muffin cups two-thirds full and bake for 25 minutes.

Brush with the lemon glaze, wait 5 minutes, then invert the muffins on to a rack to cool.

See Pg 97

fold in Blueberries

28

Rich Tea Biscuits

MAKES 1 DOZEN

These quick and easy biscuits make great shortcake, served with whipped cream and strawberries. Or simply serve them warm, split open with butter and jam.

2 cups (500 ml) all-purpose flour
1 1/2 tablespoons (20 ml) baking powder
1/2 teaspoon (2 ml) salt
1/4 cup (50 ml) cold butter, cubed
1 cup (250 ml) whole milk or blend cream

Lightly grease a baking sheet and preheat the oven to 400°F (200°C).

Sieve together the dry ingredients into a mixing bowl. Using a pastry blender or two knives, cut in the butter cubes until the mixture resembles breadcrumbs. Make a well in the centre and add the milk or cream all at once, stirring quickly and lightly until the dough forms a ball, coming clean away from the sides of the bowl.

Turn the dough on to a floured surface and knead for a few minutes very gently. Pat it out to a 2-inch (2.5-cm) thickness and cut into twelve rounds. You can use a medium-sized biscuit cutter or a small glass dipped in flour. Arrange 1 inch (2.5 cm) apart on the pan and bake in the centre of the oven for 12–15 minutes, until pale golden and dry. Transfer to a rack to cool.

Oatcakes

MAKES 10–12

These are a Nova Scotian version of traditional Scotch cakes, but the rolled oats make a pleasant addition. These can be enjoyed plain or served with butter and preserves.

1 1/2 cups (375 ml) all-purpose flour
1 1/2 cups (375 ml) rolled oats
1/2 cup (125 ml) white sugar
a pinch of baking soda
1 teaspoon (5 ml) sea salt
1/2 cup (125 ml) vegetable shortening
1/2 cup (125 ml) butter
1/8 cup (approx.) cold water, to mix

Preheat the oven to 275°F (140°C).

Combine the dry ingredients in a large mixing bowl and blend in the shortening and butter. Mix in about 1/8 cup of cold water, to form a soft dough. Knead gently and press the dough down on to a lightly floured baking sheet. Roll out to a 1 1/2-inch (4-cm) thick rectangle, and using a sharp knife or cookie cutter, cut in squares or rounds. Bake for 45 minutes. Allow to cool before storing at room temperature in a tin with a tightly-fitting lid.

Hermits

MAKES 9–12

These squares are rich with fruit and moist and spicy in the old-fashioned tradition.

1/2 cup (125 ml) butter, softened
1/2 cup (125 ml) soft vegetable shortening
1 1/2 cups (375 ml) brown sugar
3 eggs, beaten
2 cups (500 ml) all-purpose flour
1/2 teaspoon (2 ml) baking powder
1 teaspoon (5 ml) baking soda
1/2 teaspoon (2 ml) ground cinnamon
1/2 teaspoon (2 ml) ground cloves
1 cup (250 ml) chopped dates
1 cup (250 ml) chopped walnuts
1 cup (250 ml) raisins

Grease and flour a 10 x 15-inch (25 x 38-cm) jelly-roll pan. Preheat the oven to 325°F (170°C).

Cream together the butter, shortening, and sugar in a large mixing bowl until light and fluffy. Gradually beat in the eggs, a tablespoon at a time. Sieve together the flour, soda, and spices, and stir in to mix well. Fold in the dates, nuts, and raisins.

Spread the batter evenly in the prepared pan and bake for 25–30 minutes, until firm and dry. Cool before cutting into squares.

Raisin Crumbles

MAKES 1 DOZEN

These squares make a nice change from date squares.

1 cup (250 ml) brown sugar
2 1/2 cups (625 ml) rolled oats
1 cup (250 ml) all-purpose flour
1 teaspoon (5 ml) baking soda
1 teaspoon (5 ml) salt
1/2 cup (125 ml) butter, cubed
1/2 cup (125 ml) vegetable shortening

For the filling:
1/2 cup (125 ml) white sugar
1 tablespoon (15 ml) grated orange zest
1/2 cup (125 ml) freshly squeezed orange juice
4 tablespoons (60 ml) all-purpose flour
3/4 cup (175 ml) cold water
2 cups (500 ml) dark seedless raisins

Grease and flour a 9-inch (23-cm) square pan and preheat the oven to 350°F (180°C).

Combine the filling ingredients in a saucepan and cook over a double boiler, stirring frequently, until thickened. Remove from the heat and set aside to cool.

Meanwhile, in a large bowl, mix together the sugar, rolled oats, flour, soda, and salt in a bowl. Quickly rub in the butter and shortening, using your fingers, until combined. Press half the mixture into the prepared baking pan. Spread the filling evenly over top, then cover with the remaining oatmeal mixture, pressing it out gently but evenly. Bake for 30 minutes. Allow to cool before cutting into squares.

Poppy Seed Cake

SERVES 6

This cake has the most marvellous texture, and is the perfect accompaniment to a cup of Earl Grey tea. Soak the poppy seeds in the buttermilk before you go to bed, and it will be ready to use the next day.

1 cup (250 ml) butter, softened

1 1/2 cups (375 ml) white sugar

4 large eggs, beaten

2 1/2 cups (625 ml) all-purpose flour

2 teaspoons (10 ml) baking powder

1/2 cup (125 ml) poppy seeds, soaked overnight in 1 cup (250 ml) buttermilk

1 teaspoon (5 ml) vanilla

1/3 cup (80 ml) brown sugar

2 teaspoons (10 ml) ground cinnamon

For the lemon glaze:

1/3 cup (80 ml) freshly squeezed lemon juice mixed with 3/4 cup (175 ml) icing sugar

Grease and flour a 9-inch (23-cm) tube pan and preheat the oven to 350°F (180°C).

In a large bowl, cream together the butter and sugar until light and fluffy. Gradually add the eggs, beating well after each addition, until the batter is thick and creamy. Sieve together the flour and baking powder and fold in, alternating with the poppy seeds and buttermilk. Add the vanilla.

In a small bowl, mix together the brown sugar and cinnamon. Spoon half the batter into the prepared tube pan and sprinkle with the cinnamon sugar. Spoon in the remaining batter and smooth the top.

Bake for 1 hour, until the cake springs back when pressed gently. Leave in the pan for 10 minutes, then carefully invert on to a rack and drizzle with the lemon glaze.

Blueberry-Lemon Loaf

MAKES 1 LOAF

Blueberries grow wild in Nova Scotia, and there are many local recipes featuring them. Lemon perfectly complements their flavour, and this simple glaze helps to keep the cake moist.

1/2 cup (125 ml) butter, softened

1 cup (250 ml) white sugar

2 eggs, beaten

1 1/2 cups (375 ml) all-purpose flour

1 teaspoon (5 ml) baking powder

1/2 cup (125 ml) whole milk

1 cup (250 ml) fresh or frozen blueberries

grated zest of 1 lemon

1/2 cup (125 ml) chopped pecans

For the glaze:

freshly squeezed juice of 1 lemon mixed with 1/2 cup (125 ml) icing sugar

Grease and flour a 5 x 9-inch (13 x 23-cm) loaf pan and preheat the oven to 350°F (180°C).

In a large bowl, cream together the butter and sugar until light and fluffy. Gradually add the eggs, beating well after each addition, until the batter is thick and creamy. Sieve together the flour and baking powder and fold in, alternating with the milk. Gently fold in the blueberries, lemon zest, and chopped pecans.

Spoon the batter into the prepared loaf pan and bake for 50 minutes, until the cake springs back when pressed gently. Leave in the pan for 10 minutes, then carefully invert on a rack and drizzle with lemon glaze.

Poached Halibut

SERVES 4–6

Another "company" classic that both friends and family will love.

2 tablespoons (25 ml) butter
1/3 cup (80 ml) finely chopped onion
1/3 cup (80 ml) finely chopped celery
4 cups (1 L) water
1/4 cup (50 ml) freshly squeezed lemon juice
1 teaspoon (5 ml) sea salt
1/2 teaspoon (2 ml) peppercorns
1 pound (500 g) fresh halibut steaks
finely chopped fresh parsley, to garnish

For the sauce:

1/4 cup (50 ml) butter
2 shallots, chopped very fine
4 tablespoons (60 ml) all-purpose flour
poaching liquid from the fish
1/2 cup (125 ml) heavy cream
sea salt and freshly ground black pepper
2 egg yolks, beaten

Heat the 2 tablespoons of butter over a medium heat in a large skillet or deep frying-pan. Add the onion and celery and sauté for a few minutes. Add the water, lemon juice, salt, and peppercorns. Simmer for 5 minutes and then bring to a low boil.

Lower the fish into the liquid, turn down the heat, cover and simmer for 5 minutes, until the fish is opaque. Remove the fish from the poaching liquid and transfer to a serving platter in a warm oven. Reserve the poaching liquid.

To make the sauce, melt the 1/4 cup butter over a medium–low heat in a saucepan. Add the shallots and sauté until translucent but not browned. Whisk in the flour to blend well. Cook over a low heat, stirring constantly, for about 4 minutes.

Add the reserved poaching liquid and cook, stirring constantly, until thickened and smooth. Lower the heat and add the egg yolks, stirring constantly for 2 minutes. Do not boil.

Pour the sauce over the warm halibut steaks, sprinkle with a little parsley and serve at once.

See Pg 97

34

Baked Sole with Spinach and Cheese Sauce

SERVES 6–8

This creamy sauce with satisfy both sole and soul. Adding a pinch of mustard to cheese sauces brings out the flavour of the cheese.

2 pounds (1 kg) de-boned sole or haddock fillets
10 ounces (300 g) fresh spinach, cooked and drained well

1 medium-sized onion, chopped finely

1/2 teaspoon (2 ml) each sea salt and freshly ground black pepper.

For the sauce:

4 tablespoons (60 ml) butter

4 tablespoons (60 ml) flour

2 cups (500 ml) milk

1/4–1/2 teaspoon (1–2 ml) dry mustard

1 teaspoon (5 ml) sea salt

1/8 teaspoon (.5 ml) freshly ground black pepper

1/4 cup (50 ml) grated sharp Cheddar cheese

To make the sauce, melt the butter in a small saucepan over a medium–low heat. Add the flour and cook for a few minutes, stirring constantly. Gradually add the milk, stirring constantly. Season with the dry mustard and salt and pepper. Stir in the grated cheese and cook over a gentle heat for about 10 minutes more, until the sauce is smooth and thickened.

Meanwhile, generously butter a baking dish and preheat the oven to 425°F (220°C). Arrange half the fish fillets in the buttered dish and cover with all of the cooked and drained spinach. Scatter the chopped onion over top and season with salt and pepper. Cover with the remaining fish and pour the sauce evenly over top. Bake for 20–30 minutes, uncovered, until the fish is opaque and flakes easily when prodded with a fork. Serve at once.

Baked Haddock Fillets with Crunchy Almonds

SERVES 6–8

This is one of my favourite haddock recipes, and it's so easy to make that I often invite friends to share it. You can substitute halibut or scallops.

1 1/2 pounds (750 g) fresh haddock fillets, bones removed

1 1/2 cups (375 ml) whipping cream or low-fat plain yoghurt

1 1/2 cups (375 ml) fine dried breadcrumbs, seasoned with salt and white pepper

1/3 cup (80 ml) freshly squeezed lemon juice

1 cup (250 ml) slivered almonds, sautéed in 3 tablespoons (40 ml) butter

1/2 cup (125 ml) finely chopped fresh parsley and 1 sweet red pepper, seeded and sliced in slivers, to garnish

Lightly butter a 9 x 13-inch (23 x 33-cm) baking dish and preheat the oven to 450°F (230°C).

Slice the fillets in half lengthways. Have the cream or yoghurt and breadcrumbs ready in two separate shallow dishes. Dip the fillets first in the cream or yoghurt, then in the breadcrumbs. Roll up the fillets pinwheel fashion. Arrange in the prepared baking dish and drizzle with the lemon juice and the remaining cream or yoghurt.

Bake on the lowest oven rack for about 15 minutes, until the fish is opaque. Don't overcook the fish as it quickly goes from being "just right" to dry and tough. Then remove the fish from the oven and sprinkle with the sautéed almonds. Place under the broiler for just a few minutes, until golden-brown.

Sprinkle with the parsley and red pepper and serve at once.

Poached Salmon

SERVES 8–10

Atlantic salmon are moist and flavourful, and a whole poached fish makes a wonderful meal for guests. It looks spectacular but is so easy and quick to prepare.

3–5 pound (1.5–2.5 kg) whole salmon, rinsed and patted dry
sea salt
1/2 cup (125 ml) freshly squeezed lemon juice salad greens and thinly sliced red, yellow, and green sweet peppers, to garnish

Fill a fish kettle or large shallow pan (with a rack insert) with water. Bring to a simmer.

Meanwhile, generously butter a large piece of heavy foil. Place the salmon in the centre of the foil and fold the edges firmly up against the fish. Sprinkle the fish with salt and pour the lemon juice evenly over top. Pinch the foil closed and seal tightly.

Carefully lower the wrapped fish into the simmering water. Cover the kettle or pan, reduce the heat to minimum, and simmer very gently for about 40 minutes (10 minutes per 1-inch thickness of fish). The fish is done when it is opaque and flakes easily when prodded gently with a fork.

Remove the foil and skin the fish, using a sharp knife. Transfer to a large serving platter and garnish with salad greens and thin slivers of colourful sweet pepper.

Fish-Cakes

SERVES 6

A true Nova Scotian tradition, everyone loves fish-cakes. These are great served with home-made baked beans and crunchy coleslaw.

1 pound (500 g) salt cod
6 medium-sized potatoes, peeled and chopped
2 large onions, chopped finely
1 egg, beaten
1 cup (250 ml) finely chopped fresh parsley
sea salt and freshly ground black pepper, to taste

Soak the salt cod overnight in cold water. The next day, remove the skin and bones and rinse well.

Simmer the fish and potatoes together for about 10 minutes, or until the potatoes are soft. Drain well and mash together. Mix in the chopped onion, egg, and parsley. Season to taste and form into patties.

Fry them in butter or oil until golden-brown and crisp on both sides.

Meat
and Poultry

Although Nova Scotia is naturally renowned for its fish, our rolling green fields provide a perfect pasture for sheep, making local lamb lovers very happy indeed. Lebanese dishes often feature lamb, whose robust flavour perfectly complements Middle Eastern spices.

Fatayir (Delicious Pocket Breads)

MAKES ABOUT 4 DOZEN

Fatayir is essentially a soft bread dough stuffed with meat or vegetable fillings before being baked. It is one of the most popular Lebanese appetisers and makes a complete light meal if served with a salad. These freeze very well.

For the dough:

2 cups (500 ml) scalded milk

2 cups (500 ml) cold water

1 tablespoon (15 ml) sugar

2 tablespoons (25 ml) dry yeast

2 eggs, beaten

1/2 cup (125 ml) canola oil

1/2 cup (125 ml) butter, softened

2 tablespoons (25 ml) sea salt

10–12 cups (2.5–3 L) all-purpose flour

For the Potato and Lamb Filling, mix together:

2 pounds (1 kg) boneless lamb or cross-rib roast, ground coarsely

6 medium-sized onions, chopped finely

2 cups (500 ml) finely chopped celery

1 teaspoon (5 ml) sea salt

1/2 teaspoon (2 ml) freshly ground black pepper

3/4 cup (175 ml) tomato ketchup

6 large potatoes, grated and squeezed dry

For the Spinach and Feta Filling, mix together:

2 pounds (1 kg) fresh spinach or Swiss chard, rinsed, dried and chopped finely

1/2 pound (250 g) feta cheese, crumbled (optional)

6 medium-sized onions, chopped finely

1/2 cup (125 ml) freshly squeezed lemon juice

1/2 cup (125 ml) extra virgin olive oil

1 teaspoon (5 ml) sea salt

1/2 teaspoon (2 ml) freshly ground black pepper

Combine the milk, water, and sugar in a large bowl and allow to cool until lukewarm. Sprinkle the yeast over top and leave for 5–10 minutes to proof. Stir in the egg, oil, butter, salt and two cups of flour, beating until combined. Gradually add the remaining flour, until a soft dough is formed.

Turn it out on to a lightly floured surface and knead for 4 minutes. Form the dough into a ball and place in a lightly greased bowl, seam-side down. Cover with a clean cloth and leave in a warm place to rise until doubled in bulk (1 1/2–2 hours).

Meanwhile, make the filling (see recipes above), preheat the oven to 450°F (230°C), and lightly grease a baking sheet.

Punch down the dough to release the air pockets. Divide the dough in 4 pieces and roll between your hands to form long, slender cylinders. Break or cut off pieces of dough roughly the size of an egg and flatten them into rounds, 3–4 inches (8–10-cm) in diameter and 1/4-inch (2-cm) thick. Place a quarter cup of filling on each round, folding over the edges to form a triangle, and pinching them to seal.

Place the filled pockets on the prepared baking sheet and bake on the lowest rack of the oven for about 10 minutes, until the undersides are golden-brown. Transfer the sheet to the highest rack and bake for 10 minutes more. Remove from the oven and transfer to cooling racks.

Persian Lamb with Red Kidney Beans

SERVES 6–8

This is a meal fit for a queen—with leftovers for the king! Serve this with rice and a green salad.

2 tablespoons (25 ml) extra virgin olive oil
2 tablespoons (25 ml) butter
1 1/2 pounds (750 g) boneless lamb with fat removed, cut in 1 1/2-inch (4-cm) cubes
2 large onions, chopped finely
3 garlic cloves, chopped very finely
2 cups (500 ml) finely chopped fresh parsley
1 cup (250 ml) water
grated zest of 1 lemon
1/2 teaspoon (2 ml) ground cinnamon
1/2–1 teaspoon (2–5 ml) dried mint
1/2 teaspoon (2 ml) sea salt
1/4 teaspoon (1 ml) cayenne pepper
1 x 19-ounce (540 ml) can of kidney beans, rinsed and drained

Heat the oil and butter in a large, heavy-based skillet over a medium–high heat, and brown the lamb evenly. Remove from the pot using a slotted spoon and set aside. Add the onions and garlic and sauté for 5 minutes, until golden-brown. Stir in the parsley and cook, stirring frequently, until it turns dark green. Add the water, lemon zest, cinnamon, dried mint, and salt and cayenne pepper.

Return the lamb to the skillet, cover and simmer for 30 minutes.

Add the kidney beans and cook for 10 minutes more, until the meat is tender. Season to taste and serve.

Lebanese Yaknee

SERVES 6–8

This Middle Eastern treasure has a thousand variations. You can use all lamb, chicken, or beef, or a mixture of two or more. Try substituting lightly sautéed eggplant and zucchini for the carrots and green beans given in this recipe version. Whatever you choose, serve with fluffy white rice.

1 tablespoon (15 ml) butter

1 tablespoon (15 ml) olive oil

3 shoulder lamb chops, trimmed of fat and cut in half

3 skinless chicken breasts, cut in half— or 3 leg quarters

4 large onions, chopped finely

2 garlic cloves, crushed

1/2 teaspoon (2 ml) cayenne pepper— or 1 jalapeño pepper, chopped finely

1/2 teaspoon (2 ml) ground cinnamon

1 cup (250 ml) beef consommé

1 x 19-ounce (540-ml) can of stewed tomatoes, puréed

1 pound (500 g) fresh green beans, trimmed

1 cup (250 ml) thinly sliced carrot "coins"

1 x 19-ounce (540-ml) can of lima beans, rinsed and drained

1 x 19-ounce (540-ml) can of chickpeas, rinsed and drained

chopped fresh parsley and thinly sliced sweet red pepper, to garnish

Heat the butter and oil in a large, heavy-based skillet over a medium–high heat and slowly brown the lamb and chicken all over. Remove the meat using a slotted spoon. Add the onions and garlic and sauté for about 5 minutes, until softened and golden. Return the meat to the pan and add the cayenne pepper and cinnamon. Cook for 1 minute, stirring frequently. Add the consommé and tomatoes, including the juices. Bring to a boil, then lower the heat and simmer for 20–25 minutes, until the meat is tender.

Add the vegetables, lima beans, and chickpeas and cook for 5 minutes more. Serve on a bed of rice, garnished with the parsley and sweet red pepper.

Basic Koobie

SERVES 6

3/4 cup (175 ml) fine bulgur wheat

2 cups (500 ml) extra-lean finely ground lamb or beef

1 large onion, shredded

1 teaspoon (5 ml) sea salt

1/2 teaspoon (2 ml) freshly ground black pepper

1 teaspoon (5 ml) ground cinnamon

1 teaspoon (5 ml) dried mint

1/3 cup (80 ml) cold water

1/3 cup (80 ml) extra-virgin olive oil

Place the bulgur wheat in a bowl and cover with cold water. Leave to soak for 5 minutes, then drain well, squeezing the bulgur between your hands to remove the excess moisture.

Return to the bowl and add everything but the olive oil. Knead the mixture together, rinsing your hands occasionally in cold water. Lastly, work in the oil. The koobie is now ready to use. It can simply be shaped into patties and fried in oil, then served in pita breads, with yoghurt, green onions, and chopped tomatoes as garnish.

Alternatively, use the koobie mixture in one of the recipes to follow.

Stuffed Grape Leaves

SERVES 6–8

This recipe takes a little time and patience, but your efforts will be well rewarded. Stuffed grape leaves make a wonderful appetiser or side-dish, whether you choose to use ground meat for the filling or opt for a vegetarian version. Use grape leaves that are green, not white, on the undersides. Grape leaves are best picked before the end of July, or you can buy them preserved year-round. If you use preserved leaves, rinse them several times and let them soak overnight in cold water.

50 grape leaves

1/4 cup (50 ml) freshly squeezed lemon juice

1/4 cup (50 ml) olive oil

1 teaspoon (5 ml) sea salt

3 garlic cloves, peeled

For the meat filling:

1 pound (500 g) coarsely ground lamb or beef

1 cup (250 ml) Basmati rice, rinsed well, soaked in boiling water for 30 minutes and drained

1/4 cup (50 ml) freshly squeezed lemon juice

3–4 garlic cloves, chopped finely

1 teaspoon (5 ml) dried mint

1 teaspoon (5 ml) ground cinnamon

1 teaspoon (5 ml) sea salt

1/2 teaspoon (2 ml) freshly ground black pepper

To garnish:

parsley sprigs

lemon wedges

thinly sliced red pepper

Mix together the filling ingredients. If you prefer a vegetarian filling, simply omit the ground meat and double the quantity of Basmati rice. Add 3/4 cup extra-virgin olive oil and 1 cup each of finely chopped parsley and green onions. Season as the meat filling, adding a little extra cinnamon.

You'll need a large pot with a shallow rack insert. Even better, use meat bones, grapevine branches, or stalks of rhubarb to serve as a rack, which will add extra flavour to the stuffed leaves.

To wrap the grape leaves, place them dull sides up with the stems towards you. Place a teaspoon of filling near the base of each leaf, spreading it across its width. Roll the leaves tightly into "cigars," tucking one end in. Place the rolled leaves in the pot, arranging them closely together, alternating the direction of each row. Add enough water to come just halfway up the full level of the wrapped leaves. Season the water with the lemon juice, olive oil, salt, and garlic cloves. Weight the rolled leaves down with an inverted plate, and then cover and simmer gently for about 1 hour, until the stuffed grape leaves are tender when prodded gently with a fork.

Carefully remove them from the pot, using a slotted spoon, and arrange on a large serving platter, garnished with some sprigs of parsley, lemon wedges, and red pepper slices. Serve with fresh pita bread and yoghurt cheese or hummus.

Stuffed Koobie Patties

SERVES 8

Refer to recipe Basic Koobie (Left)

For the filling:

1/3 cup (80 ml) butter
3 medium-sized onions, chopped finely
1/2 cup (125 ml) pine nuts or chopped walnuts
1/2 pound (250 g) extra-lean ground lamb
or beef (optional)
1/2 teaspoon (2 ml) ground cinnamon
sea salt and freshly ground black pepper, to taste
olive oil, for shallow-frying

Melt the butter in a frying-pan and sauté the onions until softened and translucent. Add the nuts and sauté gently until golden-brown. Remove from the pan using a slotted spoon, transfer to a bowl and set aside. Add the ground meat to the frying-pan and brown all over. Season with cinnamon, salt and pepper, and then add to the onion and nut mixture. Stir well to combine.

Meanwhile, shape the basic koobie mixture into egg-sized "footballs," and use your index finger to hollow out one end. Fill the cavity with the onion, nut and meat mixture, then seal the end and press the ball into a patty. Repeat until all the koobie mixture and filling is used up.

Heat the olive oil in a heavy-based skillet and shallow-fry the koobie patties on each side until golden-brown and cooked through. Drain on paper towels. Serve hot or cold with yoghurt cheese and a tossed salad.

Baked Koobie

SERVES 8

Follow the recipe for Stuffed Koobie Patties (above), but instead of forming the koobie mixture into patties, spread half of it in a greased 9 x 13-inch (23 x 33-cm) baking pan, cover with the filling, then spread the remaining koobie mixture over top. Smooth the surface using a spatula or your hands, score in triangles with a knife, brush with olive oil and bake in a 350°F (180°C) oven for 30 minutes.

Old-Fashioned Stew with Dumplings

SERVES 6–8

You can make this old favourite ahead of time—like the cook, it only gets better with age.

1 tablespoon (15 ml) butter
1 tablespoon (15 ml) olive oil
1 1/2 pounds (750 g) of meat, fat removed (e.g. lamb shoulder chops cut in two; cubed stewing beef; or skinned chicken pieces); lightly dusted with flour.
6 medium-sized onions, chopped finely
2 garlic cloves, crushed
1 cup (250 ml) consommé
1 cup (250 ml) water
1/2 teaspoon (2 ml) sea salt
1/2 teaspoon (2 ml) freshly ground black pepper
1 cup (250 ml) chopped carrot
1 small turnip, chopped finely
2 parsnips, chopped finely
5 medium-sized potatoes, cubed

For the dumplings:

2 cups (500 ml) all-purpose flour
1/2 teaspoon (2 ml) baking powder
1/2 teaspoon (2 ml) sea salt
1 teaspoon (5 ml) summer savory
2 tablespoons (25 ml) butter
1 cup (250 ml) water

Heat the butter and olive oil in a large, heavy-based skillet over a medium–high heat. Brown the meat all over and then remove from the pan, using a slotted spoon. Add the onions and then sauté for 5 minutes, until softened and golden-brown.

Return the meat to the skillet and add the stock or consommé, water, and seasonings. Bring to a boil, then reduce the heat and simmer until the meat is tender. Beef will take the longest, from 45–60 minutes, lamb about 10 minutes less, and chicken about 35–40 minutes in total. Add the vegetables during the last half-hour of cooking.

Meanwhile, make the dumplings: mix together the dry ingredients in a bowl. Rub in the butter until it forms crumbs. Make a well in the centre and pour in the water all at once. Stir lightly to form a soft dough. Add the dumplings to the skillet about 15 minutes before the stew is ready. Cover tightly and don't peek!

1½ TBSP Baking powder

see pg 97

50

Easy Roast Turkey with Apple and Savory Dressing

SERVES 10–12

Our local apple season coincides with Thanksgiving, so this is a favourite holiday meal. If using a frozen bird, thaw in the refrigerator for 2 days, or immerse in cold water for 3–4 hours. Then unwrap the turkey, remove the heart and gizzards, and rinse and pat the bird dry.

12–16 pound (5.5–7 kg) turkey

3–4 garlic cloves, crushed

sea salt

paprika

For the dressing:

1/3 cup (80 ml) butter

2 medium-sized onions, chopped finely

2 cups (500 ml) finely chopped celery

4 medium-sized potatoes, peeled, cooked and mashed

3 cups (750 ml) bread cubes, toasted in a 300°F (150°C) oven for 30 minutes

2 medium-sized red apples, cored and chopped finely

1/4 cup (50 ml) summer savory

1/2 teaspoon (2 ml) sea salt

1/2 teaspoon (2 ml) freshly ground black pepper

1 egg, beaten

Preheat the oven to 450°F (230°C).

Place the prepared turkey on the rack of a large roasting pan. Smear it with the crushed garlic and season well with salt and paprika. Add 2 cups of water to the roasting pan.

Generously grease with butter, a large piece of foil and place loosely over the bird, covering the top and sides. Cook for 45 minutes, then reduce the oven temperature to 325°F (180°C) and cook for 20–25 minutes per pound. The drumsticks should be tender when pressed, and should move easily in their sockets. The juices should run clear when you insert a knife into the deepest part of the thigh. Remove from the oven and leave to rest for 20 minutes before carving.

Meanwhile, make the dressing. Melt the butter in a skillet and sauté the onions and celery for 5 minutes, until softened and translucent. Remove from the heat and stir in the mashed potatoes, toasted bread cubes, apples, savory, salt and pepper, and beaten egg. Mix well and transfer to a greased baking dish. Cover with foil and bake alongside the turkey for 45 minutes.

Cabbage Rolls

SERVES 8

Cabbage is an excellent source of Vitamin C and a good source of dietary fibre.

2 medium-sized cabbages, cored
1 x 28-ounce (796-ml) can of tomato sauce
1 cup (250 ml) water
2 garlic cloves, crushed
1 teaspoon (5 ml) sea salt

For the Filling:

2 pounds (1 kg) cross-rib or blade roast, boned and ground coarsely or chopped finely—or 2 pounds (1 kg) shoulder lamb, boned and ground coarsely or chopped finely
1 1/2 cups (375 ml) Basmati rice, rinsed thoroughly and drained
3 tablespoons (40 ml) tomato paste
1 cup (250 ml) water
2 tablespoons (25 ml) ground cinnamon
2 garlic cloves, crushed
1 1/2 tablespoons (20 ml) dried mint
1 1/2 teaspoons (7 ml) sea salt
1 1/2 teaspoons (7 ml) freshly ground black pepper

Mix together thoroughly all the filling ingredients and set aside.

Parboil the cored cabbages until limp. Drain well and leave until cool enough to handle. Peel away the leaves, cutting the coarse outer leaves in half, and discarding the centre ribs. Leave the smaller inner leaves whole.

Place the leaves on a clean working surface, place a tablespoon of filling on the narrow ends, and roll the leaves firmly "cigar" fashion, tucking the end in. Use discarded meat bones and/or cabbage ribs to form a rack in the bottom of a large pot.

Place the cabbage rolls in the pot, seam-side down, in alternating rows. Add the tomato sauce, water, garlic, and salt to the pot. Use an inverted plate to weight down the cabbage rolls to prevent them from unrolling. Bring to a boil, then cover the pot and simmer gently for 1 hour.

Transfer to a large serving platter, using a slotted spoon, and serve hot.

Roast Chicken and Rice Pilaff

SERVES 8

This supper dish is easy on the budget and delicious enough for the choicest of guests.

4–5 pound (2–2 1/2 kg) roasting chicken, cleaned, rinsed and patted dry
2 garlic cloves, crushed
1 teaspoon (5 ml) sea salt
1 tablespoon (15 ml) paprika

For the Pilaff:

1/3 cup (80 ml) butter
4 "nests" of angel-hair pasta
2 cups (500 ml) Basmati rice, rinsed and drained
3 2/3 cups (950 ml) water
1 teaspoon (5 ml) ground cinnamon
1 teaspoon (5 ml) sea salt
1/4 teaspoon (1 ml) cayenne pepper

To garnish:

1/4 cup (50 ml) butter
1/2 cup (125 ml) each slivered almonds and pine nuts
1 cup (250 ml) sliced mushrooms
1 cup (250 ml) raisins
1/2 cup (125 ml) chopped dried apricots
1/2 cup (125 ml) sweet red pepper slices
1/2 cup (125 ml) finely chopped fresh parsley

Preheat the oven to 450°F (230°C). Place the chicken on a roasting rack and rub all over with the garlic, salt, and paprika. Generously grease a large piece of foil and loosely cover the bird. Bake for 30 minutes, then reduce the heat to 350°F (180°C) and cook for 2–3 hours, until cooked through.

The legs should pull easily out of their socket and the juices should run clear when the thigh is pierced at its deepest point. Allow to cool, then skin and bone the bird. Keep warm.

To make the pilaff, melt the butter over a low heat in a large, shallow saucepan. Lightly brown the angel-hair pasta, turning to brown both sides. Add the remaining ingredients, raise the heat and bring to a boil. Reduce the heat to minimum, cover and simmer for 25 minutes, until the rice separates and swells. Add 1/4 cup water if necessary.

Just before the pilaff is ready to serve, melt the butter in a frying-pan and sauté the nuts and mushrooms until golden-brown. Add the raisins and apricots and cook for a few minutes more. Serve the pilaff on a large platter. Arrange the chicken pieces on top and sprinkle liberally with the sautéed nuts, mushrooms, and dried fruits. Decorate with red pepper slices and fresh parsley.

Desserts
and Pies

Nova Scotia's Annapolis Valley produces a veritable glut of fruit and berries, perfect for our traditional desserts and pies. Many people take advantage of the seasonal bounty to pick and freeze berries to enjoy all year long.

Down East Blueberry Grunt

SERVES 6

Good things quickly become a tradition, and this Nova Scotian dessert is proof positive of this truism.

> 4 cups (1 L) fresh or frozen blueberries
>
> 1/2 cup (125 ml) water
>
> 1/2 cup (125 ml) white sugar
>
> grated zest and juice of 1 lemon
>
> 2 cups (500 ml) all-purpose flour
>
> 1 1/2 teaspoons (7 ml) salt
>
> 1/4 cup (50 ml) cold butter, cubed
>
> 1 cup (250 ml) milk
>
> whipped cream or vanilla ice-cream, to serve

Combine the berries, water, sugar, lemon zest and juice in a covered saucepan. Heat slowly, until the juices run freely.

Meanwhile, make the dumplings: mix together the flour, baking soda, and salt together in a bowl. Rub in the butter until the mixture forms pea-sized crumbs. Stir in the milk and mix to a coarse dough. Drop by spoonfuls over the simmering blueberries. Cover the saucepan and cook over a low heat for 15 minutes (no peeking). Serve warm with a dollop of whipped cream or vanilla ice-cream.

Baked Apples

SERVES 6

Our Annapolis Valley produces a great variety of delicious apples. Serve these easy treats warm, with a dollop of ice-cream to cool the tongue.

> 6 Cortland apples, cored with skins left on
>
> 6 teaspoons (25 ml) butter, softened
>
> 6 tablespoons (90 ml) brown sugar
>
> a handful of raisins
>
> grated zest and juice of 2 lemons
>
> vanilla ice-cream, to serve

Generously butter a shallow baking dish and preheat the oven to 375°F (190°C).

Set the apples upright in the bottom of the baking dish. If they won't stand up straight, slice a thin piece from their undersides. Prick their skins with a fork or knife tip.

Mix together the butter, sugar, and raisins and divide evenly between the apples, using your finger to press the mixture into the hollow cores. Sprinkle with the lemon zest and juice and pour a cup of water into the bottom of the baking dish. Bake for 25 minutes, until the apples are tender when prodded gently with a fork. Cool for a few minutes before serving.

Fruit Crisps or Crumbles

SERVES 6

Whatever name you call them, these simple deserts are old-fashioned, but never go out of taste. If you use fresh peaches, blanch them in boiling water for 1 minute to loosen their skins, then rinse them in cold water before peeling.

4 cups (1 L) chopped peaches, skinned with stones removed

1 tablespoon (15 ml) all-purpose flour

grated zest and juice of 1 lemon

or

4 cups (1 L) fresh or frozen blueberries

1/4 cup (50 ml) white sugar

grated zest and juice of 1 lemon

or

2/3 cup (240 ml) dried apricot halves, soaked for 30 minutes then drained

4 medium-sized Cortland apples, sliced

1/3 cup (80 ml) white sugar

1 tablespoon (15 ml) all-purpose flour

grated zest and juice of 1 lemon

1 tablespoon (15 ml) butter, softened

For the topping:

3/4 cup (175 ml) rolled oats

1/2 cup (125 ml) brown sugar

1/4 cup (50 ml) all-purpose flour

1/4 cup (50 ml) cold butter, cubed

1/2 cup (125 ml) chopped walnuts (optional)

Grease a round baking dish with butter and preheat the oven to 375°F (190°C).

Mix together your choice of fruit/berry fillings. Transfer to the prepared baking dish and set aside.

Combine the rolled oats, sugar, and flour in a mixing bowl. Rub in the butter until the mixture resembles coarse breadcrumbs. Stir in the nuts, if using. Scatter the mixture evenly over the fruit/berry mixture and bake for 25–35 minutes, until crisp and golden-brown. Serve with a dollop of whipped cream or ice-cream.

Baklava

MAKES 2 DOZEN

This is a holiday treat from my childhood, when my mother made her own phyllo pastry. Now this delicate pastry is available in the freezer section of the supermarket, and we can enjoy this delicious sticky dessert all year round. Clarified butter is made by slowly heating unsalted butter for 15 minutes, until foamy, then straining it through a sieve. Make sure you don't burn the butter.

- 1 1/2 cups (375 ml) white sugar
- 3/4 cup (175 ml) water
- 2 tablespoons (25 ml) freshly squeezed lemon juice
- 1 cup (250 ml) ground walnuts or pistachio nuts
- 1/2 cup (125 ml) icing sugar
- 1 pound (500 g) frozen phyllo pastry, thawed
- 1 pound (500 g) clarified butter, melted

Preheat the oven to 275°F (140°C).

Combine the sugar, water, and lemon juice in a saucepan and cook over a medium heat for 5 minutes, stirring constantly, until it forms a sticky syrup. Set aside to cool.

Mix together the nuts and icing sugar in a bowl and set aside.

Remove the phyllo pastry from its packaging and keep it under a clean damp cloth to prevent it from drying out. Generously brush butter over the base and sides of a 9 x 13-inch (23 x 33-cm) baking pan. Take 2 sheets of pastry and brush each side with butter, then place one on top of the other. Spoon about 4 tablespoons of the nut mixture along the length of the pastry, then roll it up tightly, "cigar" fashion. Cut it on the diagonal in 3-inch (8-cm) lengths and transfer to the baking pan. Continue until all the nut mixture is used up. Brush the tops with butter and bake for 45–60 minutes. Remove from the oven, transfer to a cooling rack and brush generously with the cold syrup. Allow to cool before serving. These freeze well, but wrap them carefully before freezing.

Simple Pie Crust Pastry

MAKES ENOUGH FOR 2 DOUBLE-CRUST OR 4 SINGLE-CRUST PIES

The bad news is that you will never be able to soar above in the sky like a bird; the good news is that you can learn to make an excellent pie crust. Many people are intimidated by pastry, having perhaps produced one too many heavy, soggy crusts. Or perhaps your crusts seem to shrink away, leaving a disappointingly misshapen pie. However, you don't need to be a pastry chef to create delicious pies with a tender, flaky crust. Begin with this simple recipe, and follow my tips on rolling pastry, and you'll be amazed at your own talent. And remember, the beauty of home-made pies is that they taste and look home-made.

5 1/2 cups (1.4 L) all-purpose flour
1 tablespoon (15 ml) salt
1 pound (500 g) chilled shortening
1/4 cup (50 ml) chilled butter, cubed
1/2 cup (125 ml) cold water

Place the flour in a large bowl and, using a pastry blender or two knives, cut in half the shortening the mixture forms pea-sized crumbs. This c done in a food processor. Gradually a shortening and the butter. Sprin water, one tablespoon at a a ball.

Divide the dough in four pieces (each will serve either a bottom or top crust), cover with plastic wrap and refrigerate for at least 1 hour, until chilled.

How to Roll Pie Pastry

Place the chilled pastry on floured work surface. Using a lightly floured rolling pin, flatten the pastry gently pressing down. Now fold the edges of the pastry into its centre to form a thick square. Pull the pastry out from the centre to the edges, in all directions, to shape a circle about 1/8-1/4 inch (4-8 mm) thick and 1 inch (2.5 cm) larger than the circumference of your pie plate. Never roll back and forth. Loosen the pastry using a pallet knife or spatula and fold it lightly in half. Drape the rolled pastry over the pie plate and unfold it, easing it into the corners of the pan without stretching it. Trim the edges, leaving a 1/2 inch (1 cm) overhang. Spoon the filling into the lined plate and then roll out crust 1/8 inch (4mm) thick and 1 inch (2.5 cm) an the pie plate. Wet the edges of the bottom place the top crust over the top, pressing your fingers or a fork to seal. Bake as

1 cup ice water see pg 97

Blueberry Pie

SERVES 6

Blueberries are a Nova Scotian bounty, and there's nothing like seeing a little (or large) face grinning from ear-to-ear at the sight of this favourite pie. Serve it with a dollop of vanilla ice-cream.

1/2 recipe Simple Pie Crust Pastry (page 61)

For the filling:

4 cups (2 L) fresh or frozen blueberries

2/3 cup (150 ml) white sugar

2 tablespoons (25 ml) all-purpose flour

1 tablespoon (15 ml) finely grated lemon zest

1 tablespoon (15 ml) freshly squeezed lemon juice

1 tablespoon (15 ml) butter

Generously grease a 9-inch (23-cm) pie plate and preheat the oven to 450°F (220°C). Set a baking pan on the oven floor to catch any spilled juices.

Combine the blueberries with the sugar, flour, and lemon zest and juice in a large bowl and set aside.

Meanwhile, roll out half the pastry and line the pie plate. Add the blueberries and moisten the edges of the pastry with water. Dot blueberries with small pieces of butter.

Roll out the remaining pastry and lay it loosely on top of the filled pie, pressing the edges gently together. Trim the edges with a sharp knife, and seal the crusts together, fluting the edges with the tines of a fork. Snip a few steam vents in the top of the pie crust and sprinkle lightly with sugar.

Bake for 20 minute on the lowest oven rack, then lower the heat to 350°F (180°C) and bake for 1–1 1/2 hours more, until golden-brown. Cool on a rack to room temperature before serving.

Rhubarb and Strawberry Pie

SERVES 6

The tartness of the rhubarb is set off beautifully by the sweet strawberries. This pie has a pretty lattice pastry top, so you can peek through and see what's in store for your taste-buds!

1/2 recipe Simple Pie Crust Pastry (page 61)

For the filling:

3 cups (750 ml) chopped fresh or frozen rhubarb (1-inch/ 2.5-cm) pieces

2 tablespoons (25 ml) all-purpose flour

1 cup (250 ml) white sugar

1 cup (250 ml) strawberries, hulled and halved

2 x 3-ounce (75-g) packages of strawberry jelly

1 tablespoon (15 ml) butter

Generously grease a 9-inch (23-cm) pie plate and preheat the oven to 455˚F (220˚C). Set a baking pan on the oven floor to catch any spilled juices.

In a large bowl, gently toss the rhubarb with the flour and sugar. Toss the strawberries in the jelly powder and then combine with the rhubarb and set aside.

Meanwhile, roll out half the pastry and line the pie plate. Add the rhubarb and strawberry filling and moisten the edges of the pastry with water.

Roll out the remaining pastry on a lightly floured surface. Using a serrated pizza wheel, cut the pastry in 1-inch (2.5-cm) strips. Place one strip vertically across one edge of the pie, then a second strip horizontally, and a third strip vertically, and so on, overlaying all the strips set in the other direction, to create a woven lattice. Press down the edges and trim with a sharp knife. Seal the crusts together, fluting the edges with the tines of a fork, and sprinkle lightly with sugar.

Bake for 20 minute on the lowest oven rack, then lower the heat to 350˚F (180˚C) and bake for about 1 hour more, until golden-brown. Cool on a rack to room temperature before serving.

Peach Pie

SERVES 6

This is the ultimate summertime pie. However, it freezes beautifully (uncooked) so you can make a few extra as winter treats. Be sure to use fresh peaches, as under-ripe fruit have little or no flavour.

1/2 recipe Simple Pie Crust Pastry (page 61)

For the filling:

6 cups (1.5 L) sliced fresh peaches

2 tablespoons (25 ml) all-purpose flour

1/2 cup (80–125 ml) white sugar

1 tablespoon (15 ml) grated lemon zest

1 tablespoon (15 ml) freshly squeezed lemon juice

1 tablespoon (15 ml) butter

Generously grease a 9-inch (23-cm) pie plate and preheat the oven to 450°F (220°C). Set a baking pan on the oven floor to catch any spilled juices.

In a large bowl, gently toss the peach slices with the flour, sugar, and lemon zest and juice. Set aside.

Meanwhile, roll out half the pastry and line the pie plate. Add the peaches and moisten the edges of the pastry with water.

Roll out the remaining pastry and lay it loosely on top of the filled pie, pressing the edges gently together. Trim the edges with a sharp knife, and seal the crusts together, fluting the edges with the tines of a fork. Snip a few steam vents in the top of the pie crust and sprinkle lightly with sugar.

Bake for 20 minute on the lowest oven rack, then lower the heat to 350°F (180°C) and bake for 1–1 1/2 hours more, until golden-brown. Cool on a rack to room temperature before serving.

Lemon Meringue Pie

SERVES 6

This refreshing pie is always a crowd-pleasure.

1/2 recipe Simple Pie Crust Pastry (page 63)

For the filling:

4 tablespoons (60 ml) all-purpose flour

4 tablespoon (60 ml) cornstarch

1 cup (250 ml) white sugar

1 1/2 cups (375 ml) hot water

2 tablespoons (25 ml) coarsely grated lemon zest

1/3 cup (80 ml) freshly squeezed lemon juice

4 egg yolks

1 tablespoon (15 ml) butter

For the meringue:

4 egg whites, at room temperature

1/4 teaspoon (1 ml) cream of tartar

1/2 cup (250 ml) sugar

Generously grease a 9-inch (23-cm) pie plate a[nd] preheat the oven to 400°F (200°C).

Meanwhile, roll out the pastry and line the pie [plate,] allowing the pastry to overhang by 1/2 inch (1 cm[...] in the overhanging pastry to form an even rim aro[und]

the plate, and crimp the edges. Line with parchment paper and fill the pie shell with dried beans or macaroni to weight it down and prevent it from puffing up. Bake for 20–25 minutes in the centre oven rack, until golden-brown. Transfer the baked pie shell to a rack and leave to cool with paper and beans in place, and then remove and discard.

Meanwhile, mix together the cornstarch, flour, sugar and hot water in a medium-sized saucepan. Cook over a moderate heat, stirring constantly with a whisk, until the mixture is smooth and thick. Stir in the lemon zest and set the saucepan over a double boiler. Reduce the heat, cover and cook for 20 minutes. Stir in the lemon juice, butter, and egg yolks and cook for a few minutes more, until thick and creamy. Set aside to cool.

To make the meringue, place the egg whites in a clean mixing bowl and beat them until frothy but not stiff. Beat in the cream of tartar and continue beating until the mixture forms s[oft peaks.] Gradually add the sugar, beating c[onstantly until] [p]eaks hold their shape. [...] [mer]ingue mixture into the [...] to the cooled pie shell. [...][ge]ntly and evenly [...]e back of the spoon to

[...]0°F (200°C) on the [...] meringue is set and [...]efore serving.

Handwritten note:

Use Recipe
1/4 Recipe
Simple Pie Crust
Pastry (Pg 63)

See Pg 97

65

Pumpkin Pie

SERVES 6

This Thanksgiving classic is rich in flavour and texture. Serve with fresh whipped cream. For a seasonal variation, spread 1/2 cup of mincemeat on the base of the pie shell before adding the pumpkin filling. Alternatively, sprinkle 1/3 cup chopped pecans or walnuts on the surface of the pie 10 minutes before it has finished baking.

1/4 recipe Simple Pie Crust Pastry (page 61)

For the filling:

1 3/4 cups (425 ml) cooked puréed pumpkin
3/4 cup (175 ml) brown sugar
1/4 teaspoon (1 ml) freshly grated nutmeg
1/4 teaspoon (1 ml) ground ginger
1 teaspoon (5 ml) ground cinnamon
1 3/4 cup (425 ml) blend cream
3 eggs, beaten lightly

Generously grease a 9-inch (23-cm) pie plate and preheat the oven to 450°F (220°C).

Roll out the pastry and line the pie plate. Allowing the pastry to overhang by 1/2 inch (1 cm). Fold in the overhanging pastry to form an even rim around the plate, and crimp the edges. Do not prick the crust.

Beat the pumpkin purée with the sugar and spices in a large mixing bowl. Fold in the beaten eggs and cream, combining thoroughly. Pour the mixture into the unbaked pie shell and bake on the lowest oven rack for 15 minutes. Reduce the heat to 350°F (180°C) and bake for about 50 minutes, until the pumpkin custard is set. A knife inserted in the centre of the pie should come out clean. Cool to room temperature before serving.

Butter Tarts

MAKES 1 DOZEN TARTS

You may wish to double or even triple this recipe, as these are the best tarts you'll ever taste, and they won't stay around long!

1/4 recipe Simple Pie Crust Pastry (page 61)

For the filling:

1/3 cup (80 ml) butter
1/2 cup (125 ml) golden corn syrup
1/2 cup (125 ml) brown sugar
2/3 cup (150 ml) raisins and/or chopped pecans
2 eggs, beaten lightly

Generously grease a tart pan or shallow muffin pan (with 3-inch/8-cm cups) and preheat the oven to 450°F (230°C).

Roll out the pastry and cut out rounds to line the tart pan, using a biscuit cutter or the rim of a glass.

Meanwhile, melt the butter in a heavy-based saucepan over a low heat and stir in all the ingredients except for the eggs. Remove from the heat and set aside to cool. Fold in the beaten eggs until combined, and add raisins or nuts. Pour the mixture into the lined tart pan. Bake in the centre of the oven for 15 minutes. Remove from the oven and loosen the edges of the tarts, using the tip of a sharp knife.

Leave on a rack to cool for 10 minutes before carefully removing the tarts from the pan.

Preserves
and Condiments

Homemade preserves and condiments add a special touch to any meal, and keep the memory of harvest-time all year long.

Mustard Cauliflower Pickles

MAKES ABOUT 10 PINTS

These crisp pickles have a wonderful sweet-and-sour flavour, and are a fabulous way to take advantage of summer's bountiful cauliflower crops.

6 medium-sized cauliflower heads, cut in small florets

3 pounds (1.5 kg) onions, chopped finely

1 cup (250 ml) sea salt

4 sweet red peppers, seeded and chopped

4 cups (1 L) white vinegar

1 cup (250 ml) water

2 cups (500 ml) flour

1 cup (250 ml) dry mustard

3 tablespoons (40 ml) celery seed

2 teaspoons (10 ml) mustard seed

1 tablespoon (15 ml) turmeric

2 teaspoons (10 ml) salt

8 cups (2 L) white sugar

In a large saucepan, combine the cauliflower florets, chopped onions, and the cup of coarse salt. Cover with cold water and leave to soak overnight. Heat slowly to bring to a scald, but do not let the water boil. Drain thoroughly, then rinse and drain again. Stir in the red pepper and set aside.

In another large saucepan, mix the vinegar, water, and flour into a smooth paste. Add the remaining ingredients and bring to a simmer, stirring constantly, until slightly thickened. Taste and adjust the flavour, adding extra sugar if necessary.

Add the drained vegetables to the sauce and heat through, but do not boil. Bottle in sterilised jars and seal airtight.

Green Tomato Chow Chow

MAKES ABOUT 8 PINTS

This is a terrific way to make use of either an early tomato crop, or those which won't ripen before the first frost. Chow Chow is delicious served with baked beans or Sunday roasts.

1 peck of green tomatoes, chopped coarsely

8 pounds (4 kg) onions, chopped

1 cup (250 ml) sea salt

1 quart cider vinegar

2 hot red peppers, seeded and chopped finely

2 packages of pickling spices, tied in a square of cheesecloth

10 cups (2.5 L) white sugar

Combine the chopped tomatoes and onions in a large pot with the coarse salt. Cover with cold water and leave overnight to soak. Drain thoroughly, and then rinse and drain again. Add the vinegar, chopped peppers and pickling spices, tied in cheesecloth. Simmer for 2 hours over a medium-low heat, then drain and discard half the liquid. Stir in the sugar and simmer for 1 hour more. Taste and adjust the flavour, adding more sugar if necessary. Bottle while still hot in sterilised jars and seal airtight.

Spicy Pickled Beets

MAKES ABUT 8 PINTS

This old-fashioned favourite makes a welcome addition to any table.

4 pounds (2 kg) beets, washed

2 peeled garlic cloves per jar

2 cups (500 ml) water

2 cups (500 ml) vinegar

2 cups (500 ml) white sugar

1 teaspoon (5 ml) salt

1 1/2 teaspoons (7 ml) whole allspice

1/2 cup (125 ml) whole cloves, tied in a square of cheesecloth

Boil the beets until tender and then blanch them in cold water. When cool enough to handle, peel and slice. Place in sterilised jars along with 2 peeled garlic cloves per jar.

In a large saucepan, bring the water, vinegar, sugar, salt, allspice, and bag of cloves to the boil. Simmer briskly for 5 minutes, then discard the bag of cloves. Cover the beets with the hot brine and then "burp" the beets by inserting a straw down the sides of the bottles to remove any trapped air. Seal airtight.

Blueberry Conserve

MAKES ABOUT 3 QUARTS

Enjoy this on toast for breakfast, or dollop over vanilla ice-cream or a tasty dessert.

- 10 cups (1.5 L) fresh or frozen blueberries
- 4 oranges, seeded and chopped very finely
- 1 lemon, seeded and chopped very finely
- 1 cup (250 ml) white sugar for each cup (250 ml) of prepared fruit
- 2–3 ounces (60–90 g) fruit pectin

Combine the blueberries, oranges, lemon and sugar in a large saucepan or jam kettle and bring to a boil. Simmer for 30 minutes, then stir in the fruit pectin, stirring well to combine. Transfer to hot, sterilised jars and seal airtight.

Pickled White Turnip

MAKES ABOUT 6 PINTS

This is a Middle Eastern favourite. Serve with lentils and rice, sandwiches, or whatever takes your fancy.

- 2 cups (500 ml) water
- 1/2 cup (125 ml) sea salt
- 2 cups (500 ml) white vinegar
- 3 pounds (1.5 kg) white turnip, pared and quartered
- 3 large fresh beetroot, quartered
- 1 peeled garlic clove per jar

Combine the water and salt in a saucepan and bring to a boil. Boil for 3 minutes and then add the vinegar. Keep at a simmer.

Pack the turnips and beets in sterilised jars, add 1 garlic clove and cover with the hot brine. Seal airtight and set aside for at least 2 weeks before using.

Double Fruit Strawberry Preserves

MAKES 4–5 PINTS

While this preserve is heavenly with toasted crumpets or muffins, it also makes a quick and easy filling for a sponge cake, or a delicious topping for ice-cream.

8 cups (2 L) fresh strawberries, hulled and sliced

1/2 cup (125 ml) water

6 cups (1.5 L) white sugar

3 lemons, seeded and chopped very finely

Place the sliced strawberries in a large jam kettle or saucepan. Add the water and bring to a boil. Drain off half the liquid and discard. Stir in the sugar and chopped lemon, and simmer for 30 minutes. Strain through a colander, reserving and adding back just enough of the liquid to make the preserves loose but not runny.

Transfer the preserves to hot, sterilised jars and seal air tight.

Peach Conserve

MAKES ABOUT 8 PINTS

Place a jar of this delicate conserve on the windowsill in your kitchen and watch the light shimmer through its beautiful orange colour. Peaches can be skinned easily if they are blanched first in boiling water and then quickly plunged into cold water. Use the slicing attachment on your food processor to prepare the lemons and oranges.

16 peaches, skinned and chopped coarsely

2 lemons, seeded and sliced very thinly

2 oranges, seeded and sliced very thinly

1 cup (250 ml) sugar for each cup (250 ml) of prepared fruit

2–3 ounces (60–90 g) fruit pectin

Combine the chopped peaches, sliced lemons and oranges, plus 1 cup of sugar for each cup of fruit in a jam kettle or large saucepan. Bring to a boil and then reduce the heat and simmer for 30 minutes. Stir in the fruit pectin. Bring back to a boil for 2 minutes and transfer to hot, sterilised jars, sealing them airtight.

Cranberry–Orange Relish

MAKES 3 PINTS

This relish is wonderful with roast turkey or chicken, and tastes good with toast and Brie cheese.

4 cups (1 L) fresh cranberries

3 oranges, seeded and chopped finely

1 cup (250 ml) sugar

Place the cranberries and oranges in a food processor and pulse until coarsely chopped. Add the sugar and pulse to combine. Transfer to sterilised jars and store in the refrigerator.

Appetisers
Salads and Dips

Nova Scotia's gardens and farms provide a bounty of seasonal produce. With their colourful fresh fruits and vegetables, roadside stands and farmers' markets are a welcome sight after a long, white winter.

Garden Tomato Salad

SERVES 4–6

Fresh tomatoes from the garden, with their earthy fragrance and sweet flavour, make a simple but memorable salad. You can add pretty much anything you like to vary this dish: diced cucumbers, lightly steamed (and cooled) green beans, and a sprinkling of crumbled feta cheese are all tasty variations.

6 medium-sized tomatoes, cut in cubes

2 green onions, chopped finely

2–4 tablespoons (25–60 ml) chopped fresh mint— or 2 teaspoons (10 ml) dried mint

For the dressing:

1/4 cup (50 ml) extra virgin olive oil

1/8–1/4 cup (25–50 ml) freshly squeezed lemon juice

2 garlic cloves, crushed

1 teaspoon (5 ml) sea salt

1/4 teaspoon (1 ml) freshly ground black pepper

Mix together the salad ingredients in a serving bowl.

Combine the dressing ingredients in a small jar with a tightly-fitting lid. Shake well and pour over the salad, tossing gently.

Three-Bean Salad with Mint

SERVES 4–6

This hearty salad makes a complete meal when served with a thick slice of crusty bread. You can use any mixture of beans you have on hand.

1 x 19-ounce (540 ml) can of red kidney beans, rinsed and drained

1 x 19-ounce (540 ml) can of lima beans, rinsed and drained

1 x 19-ounce (540 ml) can of chickpeas, rinsed and drained

2 green onions, chopped finely

2–3 tablespoons (25–40 ml) chopped fresh mint— or 1 1/2 teaspoons (7 ml) dried mint

For the dressing:

1/4 cup (50 ml) extra-virgin olive oil

1/8 cup (25 ml) freshly squeezed lemon juice

1 tablespoon (15 ml) balsamic vinegar

2 garlic cloves, crushed

1 teaspoon (5 ml) sea salt

1/4 teaspoon (1 ml) freshly ground black pepper

Mix together the beans, chickpeas, green onions, and mint in a serving bowl.

Combine the dressing ingredients in a small jar with a tightly-fitting lid. Shake well and pour over the salad, tossing gently.

String Bean Salad in Lemony Cumin Dressing

SERVES 6

This makes a delicious fresh accompaniment to grilled lamb, chicken, or fish. Summer flavours are available all year long if you have a freezer. Always refresh cooked beans under cold running water to keep them crisp.

1 1/2 pounds (750 g) fresh or frozen green beans, trimmed and cooked until just tender

1 cup (250 ml) sliced fresh mushrooms (optional)

1 x 19-ounce (540-ml) can of lima beans, rinsed and drained

For the dressing:

1/3 cup (80 ml) extra-virgin olive oil
freshly squeezed juice of 1 large lemon

3 garlic cloves, crushed

1 tablespoon (15 ml) ground cumin

1/2 teaspoon (2 ml) sea salt

Mix together the salad ingredients in a serving bowl. Combine the dressing ingredients in a small jar with a tightly-fitting lid and shake well. Pour over the salad and toss gently.

Cucumber–Yoghurt Salad

SERVES 6

This cool and refreshing salad makes a great accompaniment for spicy meals, or can be served as a dip with pita bread.

- 3 cups (750 ml) plain yoghurt, drained (see page 85)
- 1 large cucumber, chopped finely— or 1/2 cup (125 ml) chopped fresh dill
- 1 garlic clove, crushed
- 1/4–1/2 teaspoon (1–2 ml) sea salt
- 2–3 tablespoons (25–40 ml) chopped fresh mint— or 1 tablespoon (15 ml) dried mint—plus a sprig for garnish

Mix together all the ingredients. Chill for at least one hour to allow the flavours to meld, then garnish and serve.

Tabbouleh

SERVES 6

Nova Scotia's vibrant Lebanese restaurant culture has made this fresh and lemony salad a popular choice. It tastes even better the next day, once the flavours have melded together. Use your food processor to chop the parsley, but be careful not to pulse it into a purée!

- 1/2 cup (125 ml) fine bulgur wheat
- 1/2 cup (125 ml) finely chopped green onions
- 4 cups (1 L) finely chopped fresh parsley
- 3 medium-sized ripe tomatoes, chopped very finely
- 1/4 cup (50 ml) freshly squeezed lemon or lime juice
- 1/3 cup (80 ml) extra-virgin olive oil
- 1 teaspoon (5 ml) sea salt
- 1/4 teaspoon (1 ml) cayenne pepper

Soak the bulgur in 3 cups of cold water for about 5 minutes. Drain well, squeezing out excess water.

Toss together all the ingredients and allow to sit.

Hummus

SERVES 6–8

This is another easy-to-prepare dip that not only tastes great, but is good for you too. Try serving this instead of the usual high-fat sour-cream dips with vegetable crudités or pita chips. It also makes a terrific condiment with broiled fish. Tahini paste is made of ground sesame seeds and is used frequently in Middle Eastern cooking. It is a good source of calcium.

1 x 28-ounce (796-ml) can of chickpeas, rinsed and drained

1/4 cup (50 ml) water

1/3 cup (80 ml) tahini paste

1/4 cup (50 ml) freshly squeezed lemon juice

2 garlic cloves, crushed

1/4 teaspoon (1 ml) sea salt

1/4 teaspoon (1 ml) cayenne pepper

1/2 cup (125 ml) finely chopped fresh parsley

a few black olives or thin slices of red pepper, to garnish

Purée everything except for the garnish in a food processor, pulsing until it reaches the desired texture. (Some like it silky smooth, while others prefer it a little more granular.)

Transfer to a small serving bowl and garnish with a few black olives or sliced red pepper. Serve as suggested above.

Fresh Beet Salad

SERVES 4–6

Beets are often overlooked as a fresh salad ingredient. They are a rich source of dietary fibre, containing potassium and, of course, a lovely sweet taste. By adding the dressing to the beets while they are still warm the flavour will be absorbed better.

3 cups of cooked fresh beets, cooled slightly and sliced 750 ml

1 Spanish onion, sliced thinly in rings

For the dressing:

1/4 cup (50 ml) extra virgin olive oil

1/8–1/4 cup (25–50 ml) freshly squeezed lemon juice

2 garlic cloves, crushed

1/2 teaspoon (2 ml) each sea salt and freshly ground black pepper

Mix together the sliced beets and onions in a serving bowl.

Combine the dressing ingredients in a small jar with a tightly-fitting lid. Shake well and pour over the beets and onion rings. Allow to sit for at least 1 hour to allow the flavours to meld.

Potato Salad

SERVES 4–6

This Lebanese-style dish bears no resemblance to our typical North American mayonnaise-based potato salad. The lemon-and-oil dressing gives it a distinctive edge and it will keep well. Use fresh herbs whenever they're available as they lend this dish a wonderful fragrance and flavour.

6 medium-sized new potatoes

1 bunch of green onions, chopped finely

1/2 cup (125 ml) chopped fresh mint— or 2 tablespoons (25 ml) dried mint

thinly sliced rings of red onion, to garnish

For the dressing:

1/4 cup (50 ml) extra virgin olive oil

2 garlic cloves, crushed

1/4 cup (50 ml) freshly squeezed lemon juice

1/2 teaspoon (2 ml) each sea salt and freshly ground black pepper

Boil the potatoes in their skins. Drain and leave until cool enough to handle. Peel the potatoes, chop into small cubes and place in a serving bowl. Add the chopped green onions and mint.

Combine the dressing ingredients in a small jar with a tightly-fitting lid. Shake well and then pour over the potatoes. Toss gently, season to taste and garnish with the red onion rings. Leave for at least one hour to allow the flavours to meld. If the dressing is added while the potatoes are still warm, they will absorb its lemony flavour beautifully.

Spinach and Dandelion Salad

SERVES 4–6

Dandelion greens turn up at Nova Scotian markets in early summer, but you can also use endive, as both share that slightly bitter, spicy flavour that complements spinach so well. This simple salad packs a nutritional wallop.

1 pound (500 g) mixed young spinach and dandelion greens or endive, rinsed and dried

1/2 cup (125 ml) chopped green onions

2 medium-sized tomatoes, chopped finely

1/4 pound (125 g) feta cheese, crumbled (optional)

For the dressing:

1/4 cup (50 ml) extra virgin olive oil

2 tablespoons (25 ml) freshly squeezed lemon juice

2 garlic cloves, crushed

1 teaspoon (5 ml) sea salt

1/4 teaspoon (1 ml) freshly ground black pepper

Combine the greens, onions, tomatoes, and cheese, if using, in a serving bowl.

Combine the dressing ingredients in a small jar with a tightly-fitting lid. Shake well and pour over the salad, tossing gently.

Yoghurt and Yoghurt Cheese

MAKES ABOUT 8 CUPS (2 L)

Unless you try home-made yoghurt for yourself, you won't understand why people bother to make their own. Yoghurt cheese is a delicious substitute for high-fat sour cream. Spread it on toast, dollop it without guilt on baked potatoes, and stir it into soups as a flavour wakener. Alternately, enjoy it with fruit or berries (you can purée it to create your own flavoured yoghurt).

14 cups (3 L) whole milk

2 tablespoons (25 ml) yoghurt starter or
plain commercial yoghurt

Gently heat the milk in a large pot, cover on, in 425°F (220°C) oven for about 20 minutes. Bring it just to a boil, watching carefully, until the milk starts to foam and rise. Remove from the heat and leave to cool until you can leave your little finger dipped in it for a count of ten. If you want to hasten the cooling, place the pot in a sink of cold water.

Stir the yoghurt starter or commercial yoghurt into the milk, cover and place a blanket over top and leave overnight (or for at least eight hours). Reserve a cupful to use as your starter the next time you make yoghurt.

To make the yoghurt cheese, pour the yoghurt in a clean muslin cloth (an old pillowcase will work fine) and set on a rack in the kitchen sink over a pan to catch the drained liquid. Leave overnight or until the yoghurt has reached the desired consistency. Transfer the yoghurt cheese into a container, stir in 3/4 teaspoon (3 ml) of coarse salt and refrigerate until chilled. You can use the drained liquid to add to bread doughs, or simply discard.

Soups
and Chowders

Our chilly atlantic winters are a good reason to have a pot of homemade soup simmering on the stove. Middle Eastern soups are thick and nutritious, as well as economical.

Red & Brown Lentil Soup

SERVES 6–8

This is delicious, nutritious and easy on the budget. As with many soups, this one tastes even better warmed up the next day.

12 cups (3 L) water
1 cup (250 ml) tiny round brown lentils, rinsed well
2 cups (500 ml) red lentils, rinsed well
1/3 cup (80 ml) brown or white rice
1 teaspoon (5 ml) sea salt
1/2 teaspoon (2 ml) freshly ground black pepper
2 tablespoons (25 ml) olive oil
3 medium-sized onions, chopped finely
2 garlic cloves, crushed
1 cup (250 ml) canned chickpeas or lima beans, rinsed and drained
1 cup (250 ml) finely chopped fresh parsley
4 cups (1 L) chicken or vegetable stock freshly squeezed lemon juice, to serve

Place the water in a large saucepan, add the lentils, rice, bay leaves, salt and pepper, and bring to a boil. Reduce the heat and simmer gently for 2 hours, stirring frequently in order that the lentils don't stick to the bottom of the pot. Add extra water if necessary.

Meanwhile, heat the olive oil in a small frying-pan and sauté the onions and garlic until softened. Transfer to the soup-pot along with the chickpeas (or lima beans), parsley, and chicken stock or broth. Add a squeeze of lemon juice before serving.

Great Fish Chowder

SERVES 4–6

This recipe is refreshingly simple, and one of my personal favourites. Living in Nova Scotia, we're lucky to have fresh fish to enjoy year-round. You can add scallops, lobster, or clams to this chowder.

6 medium-sized potatoes, peeled and cut in cubes
3 medium-sized onions, chopped thinly
1 teaspoon (5 ml) sea salt
1/2 teaspoon (2 ml) white pepper
2 pounds (1 kg) boned fresh haddock fillets
1 cup (250 ml) water
3 cups (750 ml) blend—or
1/2 cup (250ml) heavy cream
1 cup (250 ml) finely chopped fresh parsley

Place the potatoes and onions in a large pot and season with salt and pepper. Lay the boned fish fillets over top and add the water. Bring to a boil, reduce the heat, cover and simmer for 5–8 minutes, until the fish flakes easily when prodded with a fork.

Don't overcook! Add the cream, parsley and reheat gently. Don't allow the chowder to boil, either now or when reheating, as the cream will curdle and the fish will toughen. Taste, season again if necessary, and enjoy!

Lobster Chowder

SERVES 4–6

This flavourful recipe always gets rave reviews. The parsley adds both colour and a wallop of nutrients.

1 large onion; chopped
4 medium-sized potatoes, diced
1 cup (250 ml) water
3 cups (750 ml) lobster meat; chopped
1 teaspoon (2 ml) salt
1/4 teaspoon (2 ml) pepper
2 cups (750 ml) light cream and
1/4 cup (250ml) heavy cream
1/2 cup (250 ml) finely chopped fresh parsley

Place the potatoes, onions and water in a saucepan. Cover and simmer about 5 minutes until potatoes are almost tender yet firm. Add remaining ingredients and heat through. Do not over cook or boil. Makes 4 servings.

Chicken and Vegetable Soup

SERVES 6–8

The fragrant aroma of this soup simmering on your stove-top will be a happy welcome to anyone who walks through the door. If you're concerned about saturated fat, refrigerate the soup overnight and skim the surface before reheating. To add an extra boost of Vitamin C, add 1 cup of tomato juice to the stock.

2 tablespoons (25 ml) olive oil

2 medium-sized onions, chopped coarsely

4 garlic cloves, crushed

6 cups (1.5 L) coarsely chopped celery

3 large carrots, chopped coarsely

12 cups (3 L) water

1 cup (250 ml) red lentils

3 pounds (1.5 kg) chicken
(neck, backs, thighs etc.), chopped

2 cups (500 ml) finely chopped fresh parsley

1 teaspoon (5 ml) sea salt

1/2 teaspoon (2 ml) freshly ground black pepper

3 cups (750 ml) finely chopped assorted
fresh vegetables (e.g. carrots, celery, turnip,
parsnip, and potatoes)

1 x 19-ounce (540-ml) can of chickpeas and/or
lima beans, rinsed and drained (optional)

Heat the olive oil in a large stockpot and sauté the onions for about 5 minutes, until softened. Stir in the coarsely chopped celery and carrots, cover and "sweat" the vegetables over a low heat for 5 minutes. Add the water, lentils, chicken, and 1 cup of chopped parsley. Season with salt and pepper and bring to a boil. Reduce the heat and simmer for 3–4 hours, stirring occasionally.

Strain the stock, pressing the softened vegetables through a coarse sieve and reserving the chicken meat. Discard the contents of the sieve and return the soup to the pot. Add the finely chopped assorted vegetables and bring back to a simmer, cooking for 20 minutes more.

Stir in the remaining cup of parsley along with the chicken meat and chickpeas or lima beans, if using. Heat through, taste and season again if necessary. Add 3 tablespoons of dry chicken stock if desired.

Vegetarian
Meals

Nova Scotia's Lebanese communities have provided a bounty of new recipes for the growing vegetarian population. We're lucky to live in a province blessed with wonderful seasonal produce.

Spicy Rice and Potatoes with Currants and Sautéed Nuts

SERVES 8

This spicy, fruity main dish is a colourful and festive treat. Basmati rice is fragrant and flavourful.

2 cups (500 ml) Basmati rice, rinsed thoroughly in cold water

3 tablespoons (40 ml) extra-virgin olive oil

4 medium-sized potatoes, peeled and cut in 1/4-inch (5-mm) slices

3/4 cup (175 ml) dried currants

1 teaspoon (5 ml) ground cinnamon

1/3 cup (80 ml) melted butter

1/2 teaspoon (2 ml) sea salt

1/4 teaspoon (1 ml) cayenne pepper

chopped fresh parsley and thinly sliced sweet red pepper, to garnish

For the nut garnish:

1/3 cup (80 ml) butter

1/2 cup (125 ml) cashew nuts, chopped

1/2 cup (125 ml) slivered almonds

1/2 cup (125 ml) pine nuts

Soak the rinsed rice in a bowl of very hot water for 30 minutes.

Meanwhile, heat the olive oil in a large, heavy-based, oven-proof skillet. Add the sliced potatoes and cook over a low heat for 10 minutes, then remove from the pan from the heat and set aside.

Preheat the oven to 300°F (150°C).

Drain the rice and parboil in a large pot of lightly salted boiling water for 6 minutes. Drain well. Spoon half the rice over the potatoes. Sprinkle with the currants, cinnamon, salt, and cayenne pepper. Cover with the remaining rice and drizzle the melted butter over top. Cover the skillet with a clean damp cloth, place the lid on top and bake for 20–30 minutes.

Meanwhile, melt the 1/3 cup butter in a frying-pan and sauté the nuts over a gentle heat until golden-brown.

Turn out the rice and potatoes on to a large serving platter and garnish with the nuts, parsley, and red pepper.

Rice and Lentils

SERVES 6

Mjudraa is nutritious and a favourite amongst my friends. The onions are the secret flavourful ingredient—fried long and slow until they turn a rich dark brown and their natural sugars caramelise. To add an extra nutrient boost, use brown rice (which should be cooked for the same length of time as the lentils).

2 cups (500 ml) green lentils, rinsed and drained

8 cups (1.5 L) water

1 teaspoon (5 ml) sea salt

1/2 teaspoon (2 ml) cayenne pepper

1/2 cup (125 ml) rice

1/3 cup (80 ml) olive oil

6 large onions, chopped

green onions, to garnish

Place the lentils in a heavy-based saucepan and add the water. Season with salt and cayenne pepper and bring to a boil. Lower the heat and simmer gently for 30 minutes. Stir in the rice and simmer for 25 minutes more, adding extra water if necessary, lentils and rice should be dry when done.

Meanwhile, heat the olive oil in a heavy-based skillet and fry the onions for 15–20 minutes, until they turn a rich brown colour and are slightly gooey. Stir frequently to make sure they don't burn. Add them to the lentils.

Transfer to a serving platter, garnish with green onions and serve with pita bread, black olives, yoghurt cheese, and a fresh tomato salad.

Baked Beans

SERVES 8

Baked beans are a Nova Scotian tradition—their fragrant aroma welcomes hungry friends and family on a cold, snowy day.

> 2 cups dried yellow-eyed or navy beans—or a mixture of both—covered with three times their volume of water, soaked overnight, rinsed well and drained
>
> 2 medium-sized onions, chopped
>
> 1/2 cup (125 ml) molasses
>
> 1/2 cup (125 ml) ketchup
>
> 3 garlic cloves, crushed
>
> 1/4 cup (125 ml) dry mustard
>
> 1/4 cup (50 ml) butter
>
> 1/4 teaspoon (1 ml) cayenne pepper
>
> 1 teaspoon (5 ml) sea salt
>
> 1/2 teaspoon (2 ml) freshly ground black pepper

If using a pressure cooker, cover the prepared beans with water to a depth of two inches. Stir in the remaining ingredients and seasonings. Cook the beans for 45 minutes, then remove from the heat and let the pressure drop on its own.

If using a bean crock, cover the beans with two inches of water, stir in the remaining ingredients and seasonings, then cover and bake at 300°F (150°C) for about 5 hours, adding a little extra water if necessary.

Serve these delicious home-made beans with fresh brown bread and mustard pickles or chow-chow (see pages 70 and 72).

Potato Kibby

SERVES 8

This makes a welcome change from the ubiquitous boiled potatoes. Served with pita bread, it is a meal in itself.

> 7 large potatoes
>
> 1/4 cup (50 ml) olive oil
>
> 4 medium-sized onions, chopped finely
>
> 1 1/2 cups (375 ml) fine bulgur wheat, rinsed well and squeezed dry
>
> 1 cup (250 ml) finely chopped fresh parsley
>
> 2 tablespoons (25 ml) dried mint
>
> 1/2 teaspoon (2 ml) ground cinnamon
>
> 1/2 teaspoon (2 ml) ground cumin
>
> 1 teaspoon (5 ml) sea salt
>
> 1/2 teaspoon (2 ml) freshly ground black pepper
>
> fresh parsley sprigs and chopped tomato, to garnish

Boil the potatoes with their jackets on for 25–35 minutes, or until tender. Drain, leave until cool to the touch ,and then peel and mash.

Meanwhile, heat the olive oil in a small skillet and sauté the onions until golden-brown.

Mix the potatoes with the fried onions, bulgur wheat, parsley, mint seasoning and kneed well. Transfer to a large platter and garnish with fresh parsley sprigs and chopped tomato.

Eggplant with Chickpeas
SERVES 6

This simple dish is full of robust flavours—onion, garlic, and tomato. Serve it with pita bread, rice, or pasta.

1 medium-sized eggplant, cut in 1 1/2-inch (4-cm) cubes

sea salt

1/4 cup (50 ml) olive oil

1 large onion, sliced lengthways

2 garlic cloves, crushed

2 cups (500 ml) canned chickpeas, rinsed and drained

1 large tomato, chopped coarsely

1 tablespoon (15 ml) tomato paste

1/2 teaspoon (2 ml) sea salt

1/4 teaspoon (1 ml) freshly ground black pepper

1 cup (250 ml) water

Spread the cubed eggplant in a large colander and sprinkle liberally with salt. Weight down with a heavy plate and set aside for two hours to drain. Rinse well and pat dry.

Heat the oil in a large skillet and sauté the eggplant until softened. Remove from the skillet and drain on paper towel. Add the sliced onions and garlic to the skillet and sauté until golden. Stir in the chickpeas, chopped tomato, tomato paste, and seasonings. Add the water and simmer for 10 minutes. Stir in the eggplant and simmer for 5 minutes more.

Adjust the seasonings to taste and serve warm or cold with pita breads, rice, or pasta.

Fresh Tomato Sauce

MAKES ABOUT 10 CUPS (2.5 L)

In my book, tomato sauce can never be to rich or too thick. This recipe can be frozen very successfully, and you can bulk it up even further with blanched vegetables or canned chickpeas or kidney beans.

2 tablespoons (25 ml) olive oil

4 large onions, chopped

4 garlic cloves, chopped

6 cups (1.5 L) finely chopped celery

2 x 28-ounce (796-ml) cans of crushed tomatoes— or 1 dozen fresh tomatoes, puréed

1 x 5 1/2-ounce (156-ml) can of tomato paste

2 cups (500 ml) chopped mushrooms (optional)

2 cups (500 ml) water or vegetable stock

1 cup (250 ml) finely chopped fresh parsley

1/4 cup (50 ml) fresh basil, shredded— or 1 teaspoon (5 ml) dried basil

1 tablespoon (15 ml) sugar

1 teaspoon (5 ml) sea salt

1/2 teaspoon (2 ml) freshly ground black pepper

Heat the oil in a large, heavy-based saucepan and sauté the onions for ten minutes, until golden and translucent. Add the garlic and chopped celery and cook for 3 minutes more. Stir in the remaining ingredients and bring to a boil. Lower the heat and simmer uncovered for 1 hour. Adjust the seasonings to taste and serve over pasta or rice.

Published by Sherman Hines Photographic Ltd.

Photography by Sherman Hines
Printed in Hong Kong.Lam

Reproduction rights available from:
Masterfile, Stock Photo Library
175 Bloor St. E.
South Tower, 2nd Floor
Toronto, Ontario
M4W 3R8
(800) 387-9010

Photographic prints,corporate or fundraising orders from:
RR 2 Newport
Nova Scotia
B0N 2A0

Cameras: Pentax 6 x 7
and Contax 35mm with Carl Zeiss T. Lens
Films: Fujichrome ISO 100

ISBN 0-929116-74-7

© 1999 Sherman Hines—photographs
© 1999 Sarah Lynk—recipes and text

List of color photographs
Photographs by Sherman Hines

Pg.6 Berwick, pg.7 bread, pg.8 Alexander Graham Bell Museum, pg.9 Grand Pre Park, pg.10 bread rolls, pg.11 Tower Rd. Halifax, pg.12-13 Peggy's Cove, pg.14 Mission Shubenacadie, pg.15 T-ring, pg.16 Canada geese, pg.17 Canada goose decoy, pg.18 Blue Rocks, pg. 19 maple leaves, pg.20 Hackets Cove, pg.21 cookies, pg.22-23 Blue Rocks, pg.24 Hunts Point, pg.25 black forest cake, pg.26 apple blossom, pg.27 Robertson Cove, pg.28 muffins, pg.29apples, pg.30 Halifax Public Gardens, pg.31 Fortress Louisbourg, pg.32 salmon fishing, pg.33 fish, pg.34 Bluenose II, pg.35 Lunenburg, pg.36 young salmon, pg.37 Peggy's Cove, pg.38 Margaree River, pg.39 top Cabot Trail, pg.39 bottom trout fishing, pg.40 free range chicken (grampa), pg.41 lamb and beans, pg.42 White Point Beach Lodge, 1-800-565-5068, pg.43 sheep, pg.44 Mahone Bay, chicken, pg.45 beef cattle, pg.46 grapes, stuffed grape leaves, pg.47 Sable River, pg.48-49 Annapolis Valley apple blossoms, pg.50 outhouse and turkey "kahuna", Cape Forshu lighthouse, Yarmouth, pg.51 Dublin Shore, pg.52 cabbage, pg.53 Digby, pg.54 apple blossoms, pg.55 lemon meringue pie, pg.56 blueberries, apples, pg.57 blackberries, pg.58 Annapolis Valley, pg.60 Peggy's Cover, pg.61 Cape St. Mary, pg.62 blueberries, pg.63 Strawberries, pg.64 peach pie, pg.65 apple blossoms, plums, pg.66 top, home of Howard Dill, Windsor, bottom Mahone Bay Market, pg.67 pumpkins-Howard Dill, butter tarts, pg.68 Cheticamp, pg.69 plums, pg.70 Habitation Museum,Port Royal pg.71 Grand Pré and Blomidon, pg.72 cherries, pg.73 Cape Blomidon, pg.74 strawberries, pg.75 peach blossoms, pg.76 Blue Rocks, pg.77 Fatayir, pg.78 Digby Pines, pg.79 top, Fort Anne Museum Annapolis Royal, bottom, Fisheries Museum, Lunenburg, pg.80 Tabbouleh, pg.81 Peggy's Cove, pg.82 Potato Salad, pg.83 Sandy Cove, pg.84 Vogler's Cove, pg.85 Lobster Chowder, pg.86 bottom, Milford House, Milford, top, Andrew and David Hines, pg. 87 Atlantic Lobsters, pg.88 Samantha and Andrew Hines, Brooklyn, pg.89 chickens, Poplar Grove, pg.90 Blue Herring, pg. 91 spicy rice and potatoes with currants and sautéed nuts, pg.92 water lily, pg.93 Atlantic Puffin, Mallard duck, pg.94 clock tower, Halifax, pg.95 left, Acadia

"Sarah makes the best buttertarts known to mankind."

Peter Gzowski, as uttered on Morningside

"Experiencing the sumptuous offerings at Sarah's table wetted my appetite to explore her Eastern cuisine, now with both trepidation and joy I've plunge into the pages to learn at the hands of a master."

Pamela Wallin, broadcaster and journalist.

"A celtic arab food fusion guaranteed to seduce your taste buds with exotic tales of the middle east and culinary strath-spey from the east coast."

Lennie Gallant, musician

"When I had lunch at her house, Sarah Lynk conjured up a stunning fish chowder and homemade whole-wheat bread so good that I saved the poppy seeds as souvenirs of the meal."

Lesley Choyce: author, TV host and East Coast Surfer.